Honor Your Father and Mother

How to Achieve Generations of Family Unity

By

Pamela S. Ellis

Honor Your Father and Mother
How to Achieve Generations of Family Unity
by Pamela S. Ellis

Printed in the United States of America

ISBN 978-1-60647-760-1

Unless otherwise indicated, Bible quotations are taken from The Holy Bible: New International Version, Copyright © 1973, 1978, 1984 by The International Bible Society, Used by permission and the King James Version of the Bible, and The New King James Version of The Bible, Copyright © 1979, 1980, 1982, by Thomas Nelson, Inc., Publishers, Used by permission, and The HOLY BIBLE, NEW LIVING TRANSLATION, Copyright © 1996 by Tyndale Charitable Trust, Used by permission.

Book Illustrations: Otha G. Ellis, Jr.
Cover Design: Luis Belen

www.xulonpress.com

Dedication

This book is dedicated to:

My mother, Ms. Willie Webb, who continually accepted me, encouraged me, strengthened me and prayed for me before the conception of this book and beyond.
Thank you, Mother!

My husband, Otha G. Ellis, Jr., who has loved, nourished and nurtured me before the conception of this book and beyond. Thank you, honey!

My children, Andrew, Annalise and Angelea, who bring delight to my soul. You are redeemed from the curse of disunity!

And all my family and friends who supported me. Thank you!

IN LOVING MEMORY OF:
My father, Russell Stevens

Table of Contents

Introduction

One day I went to the police station to report a hit-and-run incident. My two young children were with me. We were directed to a side room, where I could fill out a report. As I filled out the report I heard a man speaking with the desk officer. The man couldn't see me and I couldn't see him, but I could hear everything he was saying. Basically, he wanted honor from his son and he was asking for help with his teenage son. He wanted to know if the *police* could do anything to help him have a good relationship with his son.

The police! The police are supposed to guard us against unknown criminals. The police are supposed to guard us from delinquents. That man wanted help with his son, his own flesh and blood. He wanted help with someone that he helped to bring into the world.

Like many others that man had trouble with his child. How does it happen though? How do innocent, young children grow up to be angry, out-of-control children? How do innocent, young children grow up to be adults that dishonor their parents? How do innocent, young children grow up to be adults that do not get along with, or disunite from their parents?

How does disunity happen in a family? Is it a random case of children just happening to grow up and causing their parents grief? Is it a mystery that no one can understand? No. It is a specific result in homes all over the world that occurs when parents do not recognize that how their children turn out will greatly depend on how their parents treated them.

I know as a parent I want to protect my children from a bad, or cursed, life. Yet there were times that I realized my behavior confused my children. I saw there were times I had been selfish and angry when correcting them. It is to God's glory that I recognized these as cursed behaviors. It is to God's glory that I recognized that if I continued these behaviors my children could grow up and disunite from me. They could grow up and have a cursed life because of my behavior towards them.

With God's help I was able to change my behavior. I didn't just stop my "cursed" behavior. I was transformed to produce "blessed" behavior by the revelation of the love of God and a love for people that I received. Romans 12:2 says that we will be transformed by the renewing of our minds. It wasn't until I had applied the truth, applied the truth, and applied the truth of the Word of God that I could change my behavior.

In this book I will share with you the revelation that I received about cursed and blessed behaviors. It is the revelation of how I can bless my children or how I can curse them. It is the revelation that if I bless or curse my children, they will bless or curse others.

Now I no longer operate in the curse of disunity. I operate in the blessing of unity. I have turned my behavior from unwittingly cursing my children to intentionally blessing them. The principles of unity that I am going to share with you in this book, once learned and applied, will change your very life...as they have mine.

This book is written for parents and adult children. This is for those who want to maintain or restore their relationships with their parents, spouses, children, siblings or any family-type relationship. I encourage all who read this book to stand on the promise of God that if they and their children will honor their father and their mother, it will be well with them and they will live long in the land (the family) God gives them (Ex. 20:12).

It is not well with many families and broken relationships are a serious problem in the world today. People divorce over seemingly insignificant reasons. There are cases in which children don't even know who their fathers are. In this book we will explore what happens to people when they dishonor God and the relationship He seconds only to Himself - their parents.

Many adult children have broken relationships with their parents and are suffering with strained relationships with their own children. Some adults do not have broken relationships with their parents yet they are still suffering with strained relationships. When adult children honor their father and their mother and teach their children to honor them, they stop the curse of broken relationships in their lives as well as in the lives of their children.

In this book I discuss three components that create loving soul ties and keep families intact. Love, nourishment and nurture are three of the basic principles of keeping right relationships between people. So whether you are married or single, have children or no children, have young children or adult children, if these principles are practiced, all of the relationships in your life will be positively affected.

Healthy relationships take time to develop. Broken relationships take time to heal. Whether you need patience or whether you need healing, time is on your side. When you spend time maintaining your relationships, your children will be happy, your spouse will be happy, your parents will be happy and you will be happy.

I am not promoting quick fixes. Relationship problems don't develop overnight, and patience and healing will not develop overnight either. Healthy relationships do not develop in a small flower pot, but in a beautiful, well-maintained garden. In the end of our lives we want to hear the Master Gardener say, "Well done, good and faithful servant!" (Matt. 25:21).

The Circle of Unity

Many people sing the song, "What the world needs now is love, sweet love." The motive of love is what the world needs and it is also what our families need in to honor our parents and walk in unity. Yet it takes more than the motive of love to make the world go around and it takes more than the motive of love to make our to honor our parents and walk around in unity. It takes the actions of love, nourishment, and nurture. These three principles, which I will discuss in detail later in this book, can turn any family from the generational curse of disunity (no common goals and not getting along) to the generational blessing of unity (achieving common goals and getting along). To rightly apply these principles of unity we must understand the soulish realm of man.

God made every person with a spirit, soul and body. Your spirit connects you to God, who is a Spirit. Your soul connects you to people. It is the basis of personal relationships. Your body connects you to the environment. You can't live without a body.

Before the fall of man, man's spirit (the part connected to God) directed our soul (our feelings), and our body followed whatever came from our spirit. After the fall of man, man lost his connection to God and all he had to depend on was his soul and body. The soul, which is made up of a person's mind, will and emotions, determined what the body would do.

Before the fall of man in the Garden of Eden, man's mind thought the thoughts of God, man's will did the will of God and man's emotions enjoyed doing the will of God. Before the fall of man, man's life was led by the will of God. After the fall of man, man's mind only did what he thought. In the fallen state of man, man's life is soulish or emotionally led.

In order to operate in the blessing of unity, we must again allow our spirits to connect to God. If we are led by the Spirit of God, our souls will be healthy and our families will live in unity. If we are led by our emotions, our souls will be unhealthy and our families will live in disunity.

Your soul is influenced greatly by your natural family. Your parents have greatly influenced the way you think, how you act and how you feel. You don't choose your parents. You have to love who you get. However, you choose every other close relationship and you choose how you will relate to your parents.

Your soul governs your choices. Your soul governs the quality of all of your relationships. The soul determines the quality of the soul ties. The soul tie is like a magnet. It draws certain types of people to you and draws you to certain types of people. If you have a healthy soul, you will draw and be drawn to people with healthy souls. If you have an unhealthy soul, you will draw and be drawn to people with unhealthy souls.

The curse of disunity occurs among people with unhealthy souls. The blessing of unity occurs among people with healthy souls. The condition of the souls of the family members can affect the whole family. The condition of the soul can affect generation after generation after generation. Generations stay connected to the blessing or to the curse through "soul ties."

Keep Your Soul Ties Healthy

Picture a rope. In the nursery of the church where I work we have the pre-school children walk from one area to another area holding a rope. All is well if everyone holds the rope. All is very well when everyone who is holding the rope walks in the same direction.

The blessing of unity in a family is that everyone walks in the same direction. The curse of disunity is that a person or persons walks contrary to the direction of others in the family. The imaginary rope that connects people is called a soul tie. A person ties his soul to another person's soul by reaching out with his soul (mind, will and emotions) and holding the rope. People can tie their souls to anything, but mainly they tie their souls to other people.

Soul ties occur naturally within a family; however, they can occur within any family-type relationship in which people spend a lot of time together. Girl friends who act more like sisters than friends can have healthy soul ties. Guys on a football team who seem more like brothers than teammates can have healthy soul ties. A teacher who seems more like a parent than a teacher can have a healthy soul tie with her students.

A soul tie occurs in any relationship that goes beyond general friendship to encompass the feeling of family. You generally do not have soul ties with acquaintances. Yet concerning everyone that you want to be close to your soul will look for and receive the soul that is like yours.

Love vs. Lust

Love is at the root of a healthy, whole soul tie. Lust is at the root of an unhealthy soul tie. A young man and his girlfriend who agree to have premarital sex have unhealthy soul ties. Brothers who agree to commit crimes have unhealthy soul ties. Parents who agree to abuse their children have unhealthy soul ties.

When a family or family-type relationship is not fueled by love, it is fueled by lust. When lust feeds a relationship, the relationship is perverted. A "thing" is said to be perverted when it is not being used the way it was intended to be used.

An unhealthy soul tie generated by lust causes people to desire to control the people they are in relationship with. When people try to control or manipulate their relationships, they do not allow their relationships to develop in a healthy way. They do not "use" relationships the way they were intended to be "used."

In a natural relationship, there are going to be some disappointments. People have differences. There may be disagreements. Everything isn't going to be all good all the time. It is going to rain

15

sometimes. Still, just as it takes the rain and the sun to make plants grow, so it takes joy and sorrow to make people overcome selfishness.

In a lust-driven relationship, selfishness is the cornerstone of the relationship. The more selfish a person is, the more controlling that person will be. "Must" and "have to" are a part of a controller's vocabulary. "Choice" is not a normal part of a controller's vocabulary. A controlling person does not respect the differences in others or tolerate disappointments from them. They want it their way. They want everyone to be like them or they threaten unpleasant consequences. Lust-driven people often want love from someone instead of wanting to give love to someone.

Lust is generally a term that people associate with sex; however, before lust ever becomes part of the body, the soul has been first affected by it. Once lust does become physical the sex drive of that person is often overactive. Lust causes people to be over-active. It causes people to "want" more than is healthy for them. Psalms 23:1 says, "The Lord is my shepherd, I shall not be in want." Yet, there are people who "want" and they "want" a lot. Generally, people who have a strong sense of want in their relationships are overbearing or overpowering. When a person acts "overly" in a relationship, he is usually bringing an unhealthy soul tie to the relationship.

Unhealthy souls are wounded souls. Souls can be wounded because of abuse, neglect or plain everyday selfishness. When a person has an unhealthy soul, most often they were wounded as a child. A person can potentially carry a wounded soul for their whole lives. Once an unhealthy soul tie has been established in a person, he "looks" for other unhealthy soul ties. Consequently, as that person ages he may have never really experienced real, unconditional love. This type of person often mistakes lust to be love.

Love Sustains Marriage

Many people in today's society do not marry because of love. They may say they married out of love. Yet as divorce rates skyrocket, we can clearly see many people do not understand what love is. Therefore, they are not marrying because of love. In a divorce situation, lust is clearly the catalyst. Lust creates a strong sense of "want." Love creates a strong sense of "give." Many people do not realize that they are lusting after a relationship or even lusting after the idea of getting married. Many people do not realize that lust is at the center of why they are marrying.

Lust-driven marriages simply do not maintain the soul harmony that will produce a long, loving marriage. It takes strong commitment to give to the other person, especially when they don't deserve it or the feelings aren't there to support giving. At times like those, the relationship will be defined...lust or love?

A week or so before I got married, I was watching T.V. and I was just flipping channels when I saw T.D. Jakes preaching. I had never heard of him at that point, but now I know he is a well-known and well-respected pastor and authority on the principle of wholeness. That day he was teaching that getting married does not make a person whole. Pastor Jakes said that when a lust-driven man and a lust-driven woman marry, "the half of him and the half of her will not make a whole marriage." It takes a loving man and a loving woman to make a marriage whole.

As the illustration on the following page depicts, a married couple who is led by lust will have a broken marriage and a great risk for divorce. A married couple who is led by lust will walk in disunity. Brokenness equals disunity.

Additionally, the illustration depicts that a married couple who is led by love will have a whole marriage. A married couple who is led by love will walk in unity. In order to have unity, the married couple must be whole. If a couple has a whole marriage, they will walk in unity, and if a couple walks in unity, they will have a whole marriage. Wholeness equals unity.

Illustration 1

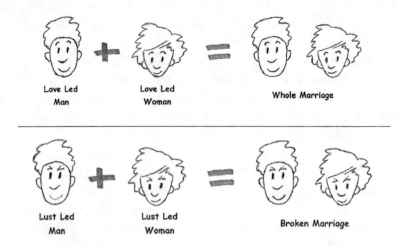

Love Led
Man

Love Led
Woman

Whole Marriage

Lust Led
Man

Lust Led
Woman

Broken Marriage

In a marriage, the Bible says the two become one flesh (Gen. 2:24). In the natural when two people get married they do not become one flesh. When a married couple has sex for the first time, they do not literally turn into one person. The "one flesh" is not a literal one-ness. It is a spiritual oneness. The intimacy that is shared in the sexual union creates the feeling of one-ness.

Sex is a gift from God and even though it is a natural act, it has natural and spiritual results. Many people are not aware that God has preset certain "things" to occur when people have sex. They are not aware that God has preset natural and spiritual results for sex.

The natural result is procreation. The natural physical actions between a man and his wife can produce children. I might add that although procreation is intended for married couples, children are always a blessing whether they are born to a married couple or an unmarried couple. There are no accidents with God. Jeremiah 29:11 in the New Living Translation says, "'For I know the plans I have for you,' says the LORD. 'They are plans for good and not for disaster, to give you a future and a hope.'"

The spiritual result of sex is the power to sustain marriages. Sex provides a couple with enjoyment with each other. Sex also provides a couple with supernatural power from God to truly unite.

Without the continual supernatural power from sex, married couples are draining out the power to become spiritually one. They reduce their marriage relationship to simply friendship.

Friends are wonderful. We all need friends. We need male and female friends. Most marriages start out as friendships. Yet when a couple gets married they are supposed to be more than friends. They are supposed to be spiritual mates for life. The sexual relationship is what separates married couples from simple friendships. When people maintain their sexual relationship, they maintain their marriage relationship.

Marriage is God's Idea

It is God's will for people to marry. It is His will for men to marry women and women to marry men. Matthew 19:12 is one reason as to why some people don't get married. They are eunuchs. They are eunuchs naturally, man-made, or have decided not to marry for "the kingdom of heaven's sake." Contrary to popular culture, there are some unmarried people who can stay sexually pure.

In a marriage the sexual union that takes place seals the soul tie between the couple. Let me stress that a soul tie had already been created before the married couple had sex. Love or lust creates the soul ties. Sex does not create a soul tie. In a marriage the sexual union between a man and his wife creates the spiritual seal necessary to sustain the marriage. The seal gives supernatural strength to the soul tie. It also gives supernatural approval to the relationship. There is like a holy "yes" over the relationship.

We have all seen the newlywed couple. They can hardly keep their hands off of each other. They have been sealed. They feel the holy "yes" in their relationship. Marriage is the highest level of relationship. It is the most intimate of relationships. After the wedding, a newlywed couple feels secure in taking their relationship to the highest level.

Before they were married, the couple is insecure regarding their relationship. A boyfriend/girlfriend is not the same as a husband/wife. They do not have the seal of approval for an intimate relationship. Newlyweds and any married couple have approval from God to have sex. Married couples have the freedom to have sex as often as they want. When married couples have sex, the role of sex is considered pure and clean. It is a gift from God.

In the Garden of Eden, God made everything good. He made everything so good that Adam and Eve didn't even know they were naked. They were perfectly at peace with their sexuality. Yet when the devil enticed Eve to eat of the Tree of the Knowledge of Good and Evil, the Bible says their eyes were opened and Adam and Eve covered themselves with fig leaves. (Gen. 3:7) They lost peace with their sexuality and felt ashamed for being naked. When they disobeyed God, what was pure in their eyes before became impure.

People Can Be Confused About the Role of Sex

Impurity is a demonic concept. Once the devil was kicked out of heaven for his disobedience, his plan then and now is to pervert everything that God ordained. He wants to pervert the purpose of sex in the minds of people. He wants people to see sex as something impure or dirty. He is deceitful enough to cause people to see sex as dirty.

When sex is committed between unmarried couples the role of sex is muddied or impure to those people. When children are exposed to sexual stimuli, the role of sex is muddied or impure to those children. When people watch pornography, the role of sex is muddied or impure to those people. When someone is molested or raped, the role of sex is muddied or impure in that person's mind.

Even in a marriage the role of sex can be muddied or impure in a couple's minds. Remember, for a married couple the purpose of sex is procreation and to supernaturally strengthen the marriage relationship. When sex is withheld, children are not produced and the marriage is not strengthened. (Even after child-bearing years, couples should not purposely withhold sex.)

There are times in a marriage when sex is withheld (I Cor. 7:4-5). However, if there are long periods of time between occasions, seek godly counsel. God gave sex as a gift to husbands and wives to feel clean and good about it within their marriage. Sex outside of marriage or sex withheld in a marriage devalues the purpose of marriage.

Marriage is Under Attack

The devil tries to do all he can to devalue God. So he attacks God's ideas to try to devalue God. Marriage is God's idea. Many people try to leave God out of their marriage. Without God they only have a form, with no power (II Tim. 3:5). Have you ever seen a car put together, but the engine is missing? Without the engine, there is no power for the car. Without God, there is no power to have a godly marriage. Without God, there is no power to maintain the friendship in marriage.

Marriage is an ongoing friendship between a man and a woman that includes a sexual union, which has been ordained by God. Married means the couple is ordained by God to have sex. Without being married or having been "ordained by God," the Bible calls sexual unions...fornication.

In recent years there has been much debate about whether marriage is only legitimate between a man and woman. There are some homosexuals who believe in same-sex marriages. There is no example of a homosexual marriage in the Bible. Marriage is only legitimate between a man and woman.

Fornication devalues marriage. All fornication, whether by a heterosexual or homosexual, is against God (I Cor. 6:9). Fornication occurs because people do not want to wait to be married to have sex. They do not want to wait for what they want. They want and they want a lot, and the media has done a disservice to the public in promoting fornication.

Still, the results of sex in a heterosexual relationship have not changed. Sex committed outside of marriage has the same results as sex committed inside of marriage. Yet the results are perverted. Instead of a husband and wife having a baby and raising that baby together, many times the mother is left to parent alone. Instead of a husband and wife creating a strong bond, many times the bond of two unrelated people is so weak it can be easily broken.

Sex outside of marriage is not acted out from a heart of love but of lust. Sex between unmarried people gives supernatural power to unhealthy soul ties. Fornication creates a false sense of security. They feel the "yes," but it is not holy. First Corinthians 6:16 (author paraphrased) says, "Even though you have sex with someone you are not married to, you have still created a seal with that person." Even if the relationship breaks up or it was just a one-time affair, those people share a spiritual seal together.

Have you ever seen a product sealed with a thin strip of plastic? The seal is in place until you open the product. There is usually a warning that says not to use the product if the seal is broken. The seal guarantees the freshness of the product. The seal guarantees the approval of the manufacturer of the product that it is OK to use the product.

Spiritually speaking, both married and unmarried couples receive the seal when they have sex. The difference for an unmarried couple having sex is that they do not have God's approval to have sex. The seal is broken.

There are a lot of broken people in our society. Although physical brokenness can occur if abuse was also part of those relationships, brokenness does not generally relate to physically broken bones. The type of brokenness I'm writing about relates to people who have broken hearts. Broken-hearted people are people who trusted their hearts and bodies to people who did not love them. How do I know that people trust people who do not love them? The relationship usually does not last. Love lasts. Love perseveres. Love is the foundation for lasting marriages.

Getting married is one of the most exciting and hopeful times in a person's life. From planning the wedding to walking down the aisle, the man and woman are full of hope for their future. Their plan is to make their marriage last forever. Yet for many their marriages do not last a year, not to mention the rest of their lives.

Some people think that marriage is only having a piece of paper, a ring and just the two of them. Marriage is God's idea and again, with God everything will have a natural meaning and a spiritual meaning. When a couple is sanctified in holy matrimony in the natural, all they have is a piece of paper and a ring, but in the spirit they have God Almighty backing up His Word about marriage.

<u>Marriage and the Family</u>

Marriage is the only relationship for which God said leave your father and mother. Mark 10:7 (KJV) says, "For this cause shall a man leave his father and mother, and cleave to his wife." There are no other relationships like a marriage. When a couple does not put other people before their spouse their unity will not easily be destroyed. The unity that a husband and wife create is like a circle. The tradition of the wedding ring is that it is shaped in a circle to represent the unity of the marriage.

Illustration 2

The graphic above depicts that the circle of unity has not been broken if the parents are married before they have children. All children born to a married couple are born in a sanctified state or legitimately. They have a head start for unity in their lives. Children born legitimately generally have a "yes" over their lives. They were born out of a legitimate sexual union.

The graphic below depicts that the circle of unity has been broken if the parents are not married before they have children. And even though children born legitimately can be unwanted, most children who have been born illegitimately have a greater sense of not being wanted. They have a greater sensitivity to rejection.

Illustration 3

Rejection is at the root of disunity. The curse of disunity begins very early in a person's life. It can begin while a baby is in her mother's womb. The curse of disunity does not begin when a person is an adult and can respond to rejection maturely. The curse of disunity starts when a person is a child and doesn't have the ability to respond maturely. Children are not mature, and when children feel unwanted and respond in a negative, immature way towards their parents, the curse is rooted in their generation.

Until children respond in a negative way towards their parents, the curse is not on their generation. When people participate in the curse of disunity, the curse is on their generation. God said He would not punish the children for the sins of the fathers or the fathers for the sins of the children (II Chron. 25:4). When children honor their father and mother, they stay under the protection and sanctification of their parents and God. When they dishonor their father and mother, they have broken unity with their parents and God.

The circle of unity can be broken at any time. Many times a parent or a spouse does not realize the circle has been broken until there is a manifestation of infidelity such as fornication, adultery or addiction. However, it is not the manifestation of infidelity that breaks the circle. It is the condition of the soul.

Families need to maintain a continual love soul tie between the husband and wife, the parents and the children, and with God. We strengthen our soul ties in our families by maintaining our deep friendships. We strengthen our soul tie to God by maintaining our deep friendship with Him through prayer and reading His Word. When we strengthen our relationship with God, our families will also be strengthened.

A family is only as strong as the husband and wife are as a couple. The children are only as strong as the parents are as a team. Marriage provides sanctification and protection for souls of the children. By participating in relationships her parents do not approve of, a child can develop a lustful soul tie on her own. However, children are not born broken, wanting lustful relationships. Broken children come from broken parents.

To prevent the curse of broken relationships, parents must keep intact 1) themselves, 2) their marriage and 3) their children. Many families fail to do all three and then not only do we have divorces, but also teen pregnancies, teen drug addiction and a host of other child-related problems.

The quality of relationships that a person has begins with his soul. However, the quality of a person's soul can affect the quality of relationships his children will have. As you read your Bible you will understand the quality of relationship that you have with God. As you read the next two chapters you will understand the quality of the relationship that you have with your parents and the quality of the relationship that you have with your children.

Understanding Your Generation

Happy Birthday!

No one remembers the day they were born. We were too tired to remember. We were too young to remember. We depend on our parents to tell us how that day went. Maybe your grandparents were present. Maybe your siblings were present. Maybe it was just your father and your mother. Maybe it was just your mother. But always remember in every situation God was there, too. God is a witness to your life (I Thess. 2:5).

You certainly can't remember when your mother first realized she had you in her womb. Maybe you were a long-awaited answer to prayer. Maybe you came too soon. Maybe you were a surprise to your parents. Yet no matter what the details were of your conception, you were no surprise to God. All life originates with God (Gen. 1:27). God knew you and He prepared for you. Still, you can't remember back to your conception.

Your memory just does not go back that far. You can't remember your conception or your birth. Your parents' memories may have also become a little cloudy as the years have gone by. Some parents don't remember the date, though they especially remember the *day*. How have they described that day to you?

Some people take pictures of the baby right after birth. Some parents capture the moment of their child's birth on videotape. Many people make a record of that day so their child can one day see what it was like on the day they were born. Parents know that child will not remember it.

In the same way, God has written a book, a record. He wants you to know that He has always cared for you (Isa. 64:8). He wrote the Bible for the times when you would begin to remember things (Ps. 119:105). You were not a surprise to God. He knew exactly what your life would be like. He wrote the Bible to help you navigate your way in life (Jos. 1:8).

Unity or Disunity is learned in Childhood

Every baby born has the potential to grow up to know God. Babies can grow up to know God, but they can also grow up to know their parents. Getting to know each other in those early days is very important in the life of parents and newborns. Babies are so sweet. Were you a sweet baby? Were you colicky? Were you a fat baby? Were you ill? What kind of baby were you? If your parents are still living, ask them. Or if you have older siblings ask them what kind of baby you were.

God put together your personality before you were even born. He knew you before the foundations of the world (Eph. 1:4). Whatever age you are now, God put everything in you to make you who you are today when you were a baby. Some people think that after a child's birth only time will tell what will become of that child. In some regards that is true. It does take love, nourishment and nurture to cause a child to become all she can be. Only time will tell how much love, how much nourishment and how much nurture a child will actually receive from her parents.

Abused children receive very little love. Neglected children receive very little nurturing. Poor children receive very little nourishment. And only time will tell how these children will respond to their lives. Some children grow up to be bitter. Many children grow up to be selfish. Some children don't grow up.

Behavior Speaks

How about you? What kind of child were you? Were you full of life? Or were you angry or sad most of the time? I know as a child I often had to wait. Good things were a possibility, but I could never quite have what I wanted when I wanted it. I remember looking at catalogs yearning for things, but not able to attain the things I yearned for.

I was born to a single mother. She later married my father, but they separated when I was about seven years old and divorced by the time I was thirteen years old. My mother was financially poor and at times she needed governmental assistance to care for my two brothers and me.

As a child, I did not complain a lot. I find that as I am getting older I am more opinionated. (I am working to keep more of my opinions to myself.) What about you? What kind of child were you? Did you always get what you wanted? Did you often get what you wanted? Did you seldom get what you wanted?

How did that make you feel? Did you honor your parents or did you dishonor them? Children develop attitudes towards their parents at a very young age. Unless there is poverty, abuse, busyness or mental or physical sickness, most children have a normal relationship with their parents. Was your relationship with your parents normal? Were there problems?

By "normal" I do not mean perfect. There is no such thing as a perfect parent. In order to be a perfect parent in the eyes of a child, a parent would have to grant the child's every desire. This, of course, is not possible. A child can have some desires that are simply not good for him. A parent cannot grant every child's desire for the child's safety. Still, a normal parent will grant many of a child's desires. Poverty, abuse, busyness or chronic sickness causes parents to be unable to relate to their children's wishes in a normal way. Children are not always able to verbally express their feelings, but you can usually understand what a child wants by their behavior. Many times children receive what they need simply by positively interacting with you. However, if a child feels unloved, undernourished or not nurtured, they will use negative interactions to get your attention. I might add as children live moment by moment they can at any time feel unloved, undernourished or not nurtured. (Don't expect too much from a hungry two-year old.)

Speaking of two-year-olds… One day while I was writing this book, my almost-two-year-old came to me with a block on her head. It is a little "Lego" type block and she thinks it's funny when she has a block on her head. When she came into the room I was preoccupied and although I noticed her presence, I didn't acknowledge her right away. When I realized that she was not just passing through, I acknowledged her. Then I saw it. She had a block on her head. This was a little two-year-old game that my daughter liked to play. So I exclaimed, "Anna, you have a block on your head!" To which she gave her usual response…giggling.

Were you a child that was noticed? Or were you always begging for attention? Did you enter adolescence with a sense of belonging or were you still yearning for someone to notice you? Your personality determines how hard you will try to be noticed. I am a laid-back person and if I talk with at least one person I feel noticed. If you are a more outgoing person, you will try harder to be noticed.

One Sunday morning I was working in my church's nursery and my coworker's daughter, although she is an older child, didn't go with the older children to Children's Church. For five hours (through two services) that little girl tried to get someone to notice her. She didn't just hang out. She wanted to be noticed.

That particular Sunday was balloon Sunday in which the Nursery gives out balloons to all the children 2 years old and up. (The nursery goes up to age 5 and there are usually 100 balloons blown up on that Sunday for the two services). The little girl rubbed a balloon on her hair to make static. To be a part of the Nursery staff a person has to be at least 15 years old and although, she was only 6, she put on a nursery smock, which is the Nursery "uniform." By her actions, she was saying, "Look at me. Look at me." She wanted to be noticed and the good news is there were plenty of people around to notice her.

If a child is not noticed, their self-esteem will be greatly damaged. Without proper self-esteem, children will not be able to value their relationships with their parents. And adolescence is the time of life when children display their value towards their parents and they also display how they feel their parents value the relationship with them. But more than that, they will show their parents how they have felt their parents have valued the relationship with them, while they have been growing up. These feelings are based on present and past experiences.

What kind of teenager were you? Did you place a high value on your relationship with your parents or a low value? Did you honor your parents or did you dishonor them? Did you trust your parents or just your friends or only yourself? Many teenagers do not trust their parents. Many teenagers try to live a life apart from their home life. They do not want their parents to supervise them. One cause of juvenile crime can be attributed to a lack of adult supervision.

<u>God Has Been Watching Over Your Life</u>

Do you know when you were born God knew how you would relate to your parents? He knew you had the capacity to go to the far right or the extreme left. He knew all the times you would cry inside because of the wrong decisions your parents would make. He knew the times you would secretly want so much more from your parents. He wrote the Bible so that He could show you that even with the best of human parents He is the only perfect parent (Ps. 145:17).

God is your Father and He loves you with an everlasting love (Jer. 31:3). You may ask, "Where was God when I was a child?" Maybe you were molested. Maybe you ate bread and drank water every night for dinner. Maybe your parents had no time for you. "Where was God then?" you ask. He has always been there...waiting for you to acknowledge Him just as my daughter waited for me to acknowledge her. She didn't just want me to be aware of her. She wanted me to talk to her.

God does not want us to just be aware of Him. He wants us to talk to Him. However, many people want to blame God for the bad things that have happened in their lives. They want to say, "If God were God, then my parents would have really loved me." Some mistakenly believe that God is responsible for everything. Technically, this is true. God is responsible in the fact that He has set up laws for human beings to live by (Ex. 13:9). Yet He has given parents as well as children a choice to live by those laws or not.

Before knowing God's laws, children know their parents and the "laws" or rules that parents set up. Children have a choice to live by those rules or not. Children have to be taught the family rules. Still, when babies are born, there are no rules. There is only one question. From the day a child is born she wants to know: Daddy, Mommy, do you love me? Although there are rules with a teenager, the teenager still wants to know the same thing: Daddy, Mommy, do you love me? When we are children we want to know that we are loved. How well we are able to show and tell our children that they are loved will be based on how loved we felt as children.

<u>Make Love Last</u>

Many people are confused about what love is. Love is the great sensation of positive feelings we feel towards others. Love is a feeling, but it is more than a feeling. It is positive treatment of others while having positive feelings. It is doing things for their good while valuing them. Some people stop loving their children, parents or spouses. They stop doing things for their family members' good. They stop valuing their family members. They stop loving their family members.

Have you been a person who has felt loved? I have been a person who has felt loved over a long period of time. I know what it means to be loved. I have been married for over ten years and I know my husband loves me. In order to have a lasting marriage, one must know what love is.

I had learned what love was before I got married. I learned it from my family. I was valued in my family and was treated positively. One reason for this is because of the birth order of my family. I am the only girl and my two brothers are 5 and 6 years older than I am. So I had positive treatment because I was the only girl and the youngest. Also, my mother was a teenager when my brothers were born, but she and my dad were in their twenties when I was born. This is not to say that when my brothers were born that they were not loved, but it is to say that my parents were older and had more natural understanding of child rearing when I was born. My parents did things for my good.

Song of Solomon 2:7 says that we should not awaken love before the time. Most young people do not understand the sacrificial part of love that comes with parenting. They are immature. They are not ready for it. However, with the third baby, my mother could more easily understand and respond to my needs. She did many things for my good.

I have been told that I was a good baby and not very fussy. I was easy to love. This is a very important point. Many children who are fussy are labeled hard to love and often do not receive the love they need. If my parents had not loved me, I would have had a harder time recognizing love. I did not go from relationship to relationship, looking for love. As I grew up my soul did not gravitate toward men who would disrespect me. I knew what love should feel like. And I believe I was divinely protected from disrespectful men because I was not confused about love.

God is Love

God is love (I Jn. 4:16). Many people do not recognize love from their parents and they do not recognize love from God. And back to my example of my daughter, if I would have been too busy I would not have recognized that she even walked into the room. Some people are so busy chasing life that they don't recognize God when He comes to them. They don't recognize His love. They don't recognize Him.

I would not have recognized God as easily as I did if I had not felt loved by my parents. While growing up my father was not with our family all the time, yet he still did things to make me believe that he loved me. Parental love makes it easier for a child to believe God loves him and be able to love Him back. However, I know many people who love God but felt like their parents didn't love them.

It is a sad fact in life that there are children who are unloved, undernourished and not nurtured by their parents. But some people, even though they may not have received parental love, still recognize and acknowledge God. In spite of parental rejection, they love

Him back. I have heard many testimonies of people who rode the church bus and received God's love from church members. I have heard of kind teachers, neighbors, grandparents, aunts and uncles who have shared love with children whose parents did not love them. Psalms 27:10 says if my mother and father forsake me, the Lord will take care of me. God will make a way to come to you and it is through love.

God is continual love. He doesn't stop loving. He is always valuing us and doing things for our good (Rom. 8:28). Anytime you have felt love, God was presenting His love through a person to you. Love is from God.

When people are in a relationship with God, they are able to love for long periods of time. When people are not in a relationship with God, they are unable to love for long periods of time. People cannot love for lengthy periods of time when they are separated from God. The human race became separated from God when Adam, God's first human son, chose to stop loving God (Gen. 2:7).

God told Adam not to eat of the tree of Good and Evil. Adam disobeyed God. He and Eve ate of the tree. Their disobedience proved they stopped valuing God. When they stopped valuing God and His Word, they stopped loving God. When they stopped loving God, they disobeyed Him and sinned (Jn.14:15). Disobedience against God is sinning against God (Rom. 5:19).

Sin separates mankind from a relationship with God. It separates you and me from receiving God and loving Him. Before we can truly receive God, we must believe that He loves us. How do we know he loves us? Remember what love is. It is valuing others and doing what's best for them.

After mankind was separated from God, He had a plan to restore mankind back in relationship with himself. However, it would take a sinless person to bridge the gap between a loving God and people who choose to stop loving. It would take someone like God who would not choose to stop loving. So God sent His Son. Jesus is the Son of God (Luke 3:22) and no one can come to the Father except through Him (Jn. 14:6).

<u>Receive the Love of God</u>

The way to receive the love of God is through Jesus Christ. For God so loved the world (you and me) that He gave His only Begotten Son that whoever (you and me) believes in Him shall live and not perish (Jn. 3:16). Second Corinthians 5:19 says that God used Christ to reconcile us back to Himself. What does reconciliation mean? There had been a separation. It means that at one time we were without God. It means that at one time we were against God and His way of living, even though He knew what was best for us. Although He loved us, we didn't love Him. We didn't recognize the value of His love for us or how to love Him back.

Jesus proved His love for us. He laid down His life so that we could receive the love. He laid down His life for our good. He paid the price for our sins to be removed so that we could have a loving relationship with God the Father. Jesus valued mankind, and what He did for us on the cross proves He loves us.

God proved He loved us by sending Jesus. We must prove that we love Him. How do we prove it? We prove that we love God by accepting that Jesus is the Son of God, who died for our sins and rose back to life by the power of God. We prove we love God by valuing Jesus and living in such a way as to bring Him honor.

I initially valued God in my heart as a child in children's church. I believed in Jesus. I felt such love coming through the man who led the group that I thought he was Jesus. But I gave my heart to Jesus with the help of my mother. It was with my mother that I first loved God back. It was with my mother that I decided to live for God. Can you remember when you gave your heart to the Lord? Have you given your heart to the Lord? Do you live for God? Do you love God?

Loving God is the starting point of the help and hope for you and your family that this book offers. How is your relationship with God? Are you sure of His love? Have you loved Him back? Your proof that you love God is that you give Jesus your heart. If you have never given Jesus your heart, or have stopped living for Him, please pray this prayer:

Heavenly Father, I come to you with an open heart. I know You love me. I want to love You back with all of my heart, soul and strength. Jesus, I believe in You. I give You my heart. I repent of my sins and I ask you to forgive me. I will live to please You. Father, thank you for helping me to love You and my family for a long time in Jesus' Name. Amen.

Loving God is the first step to truly being able to love. You have uncovered how this truth has affected you. Read on to explore how it has affected your children.

Understanding the Next Generation

A Baby!

Having a child is the kind of experience that changes your life forever. Do you remember the first kick? The first squirm? The first time you held that little one in your arms? Does the baby look like you, the other parent or Aunt Sue? Isn't it amazing how the baby can come out looking like a member of the family?

The first time I saw my firstborn I didn't notice any family resemblance. He didn't look like my husband or me at first. (As my son has gotten older he resembles my husband a lot.) The first time I held Andrew (I tell him about this from time to time) I did notice something about him. After the nurse placed him in my arms he continued to cry, "Waa, waa." I spoke his name, "Andrew." He immediately stopped crying and blinked a few times. He opened his eyes and then I saw his dimples. He wasn't exactly smiling, but he was calm. He was comforted by seeing me and I was awestruck about the comforting power that I had on this little baby right at first. Right away my baby felt my love. Love comforts others. Love calms others (Phil. 2:1).

Parents Comfort Their Children

Even though each child is different and there can be different circumstances each time a child is born, I experienced the same comforting power with my second child as I did with my first child.

I tell her about her newborn experience from time to time also. I tell her how I comforted her. The power to comfort. This power tells your children that they are going to be okay and they believe it. Did you experience comforting power with your babies?

With my first child I felt especially inadequate as a new mother. My mother came to Tulsa where I live and she had been there with my husband and me when Andrew was born. I felt a greater peace with her there. She still had the power to comfort me. What about you? Do your parents still have comforting power on you?

As our children are growing up, I realized my husband and I still have great comforting power on them. The power didn't go away when they stopped being babies. Although, the ways I bring comfort to my children now that they are older have changed. Instead of comforting a hungry baby with a bottle of milk, I comfort my nine-year-old with a Mighty Kid Meal from McDonald's. Instead of rocking a sleepy baby to sleep, I encourage my five-year-old to sleep in her bed. The comforting methods may change, but the results are the same. Do you still comfort your child?

I also realized that as my children got older I had greater expectations of them. Their comfort was not as imperative as it was when they were babies. I believe that has much to do with how I personally feel about comfort. I have had to adjust my thinking about comfort as it applies to my children from time to time because I can tend to expect them to have more grownup feelings toward comfort as I do. What about you? Do you comfort your child the way you want to be comforted?

I am somewhat of a people watcher and I have noticed how the young people in my life comfort. The teenage girls that I work with in the nursery department of my church are so kind to the little ones. I have commented to some of their mothers what wonderful girls they are raising. The girls have the power to comfort.

The umpire for one of my son's kindergarten T-Ball game was a teenager. He was very kind to the kids. I told my husband that this young man's parents must be very proud of him. He has the power to comfort. Children who are comforted by their parents grow to be teenagers who comfort younger kids. Does your teen have the power to comfort?

The Bible says Jesus was moved with compassion (Matt. 9:36, 14:14, 20:34). Compassion is the quality in us that makes us want to comfort someone. Mercy is another word for compassion. So many times we get busy with life that we forget that a baby is still a baby, a child is still a child and a teenager is still a teenager. They need to be comforted. If we take the time to comfort our children, compassion and mercy will be extended to the fullest to our children. If we take the time to comfort our children, they will take the time to comfort our grandchildren.

God is the God of all comfort (II Cor. 1:3). He is the One who tells parents that they are going to be okay. He comforts them. I believe when God chooses people to become parents He wants them to display His comforting power. His power is what is needed in our parenting and in every area of our lives.

Children Have Needs

The basic needs a child will have are physical, emotional and spiritual needs. The U.S. Department of Agriculture cites that by the time a child is eighteen years old, parents will have spent over $100,000 per child on housing, food, transportation, healthcare, childcare, education and other needs and wants. Therefore, it is important to have a good income to raise children. Are you supplying your children's physical needs or is someone else?

Because so many mothers had gone back to work in the late 1980s and early 1990s, a phrase in child rearing became popular: quality time. Although that is a popular phrase and children do need quality time with their parents, children still need both quantity and quality time to have their emotional tanks filled. When both of the parents work full time outside of the home the children will not often receive the quantity of time that they need with their parents. There just isn't a lot of time for them. Are you supplying your children's emotional needs or is someone else?

Children are very soft hearted towards God. They are often curious about God. When we train our children in the way they are to go spiritually, they will not depart when they are old. (Prov. 22:6)

Are you supplying your children's spiritual needs or is someone else?

God has a plan for your children. When I realized that God had a plan for my children I began to treat them differently. I began to treat them more honorably. I began to treat them like they were somebody else's kids. You know how sometimes you can treat someone else's kids better than your own kids. Well, our kids are somebody else's kids. They are King's kids. Do you treat your children like they are children of God?

Parents Have Parenting Styles

From the time when you suspected life inside of you—or your wife told you about the life inside of her—until the umbilical cord had been cut, you were formulating an idea of what kind of parent you would be. You couldn't see it happening, but memories of events between you and your parents rose up from your subconscious. Can you see your mother in your parenting style? Can you see your father in your parenting style?

Although our parents are our natural parental role models for our parenting styles, God wants us to model our parental style after Him. God is not harsh with His children. What about you? Are you harsh? Are you gentle? Are you somewhere in between?

All parents fall within one of the two categories with their parenting style: authoritarian or permissive. Most people are not all authoritarian or all permissive. They are a blend of the two parenting styles with one style stronger in intensity than the other style.

An authoritarian parent will be clear in his directions. This kind of parent will keep his word. This kind of parent can be harsh. This kind of parent can even be controlling. In comforting his child he will tend to believe the child needs things to feel comforted. Are you an authoritarian parent?

A permissive parent will be more flexible in her directions. This kind of parent will be very gentle to her child. This kind of parent can be smothering. This kind of parent can be easily manipulated by her child. In comforting her child a permissive parent will tend to believe the child just needs her to feel comforted. Are you a permissive parent?

As a Christian God's Word is the balance to your parenting style. Although an authoritarian parent will make a lot of the decisions for the children, God's Word will remind that parent to be merciful. Although a permissive parent will let the children make a lot of their decisions, God's Word will remind that parent to make the children obey.

Whether you are a permissive parent or an authoritarian parent, when God chose you to become a parent, He equipped you with everything you would need to love your child, nourish your child and nurture your child (Jn. 15:16). God chose you to be your child's parent.

He chose you because He knew you would have what your child needed to become everything He wanted her to be. So many times we feel so insecure in our role as a parent and in some ways we should. We are not God. Yet we can be very comforted when we know God (Ps. 23:4). When we know God we can trust Him to show us things we do not know about parenting (Jer. 33:3). When we know God we can trust Him to provide for our children's needs (Phil. 4:19). He says they are going to be okay and we believe it.

Although we are imperfect parents, we can be confident parents. Confident parents love their children. A parent may say that he loves his children, but the way he treats his children will prove whether he loves his children or not. Are you a confident parent? Are you loving, nurturing and nourishing your children?

Children need a balanced life. In my parenting style I tend to be more authoritarian while my husband tends to be more permissive. Thus, we create balance for our children. Having a father and a mother is usually all the balance that a child needs. Many people used to stay married for the sake of the children. One parent simply cannot be everything to a child. Does your child have balance? Or are you single parenting?

Balance Your Parental Style

It has been said that it takes a village to raise a child. This statement has some credibility because so many homes today only have one parent and one parent cannot and is not supposed to do it all. *Well, that may be great*, you think, *but I am a single parent.* If you are a single parent, as a Christian, you are not alone. God is with you (Matt. 28:20). Ask Him to show you how to get your child in an environment where those in authority have a somewhat opposite parenting style than you, but not opposite convictions. There are plenty of clubs, teams, and youth groups that can help fill the void in a single parent home. However, for the child to get the greatest impact the leader of that group should have a "parenting" style different from the single parent. You want your child to experience balance.

To achieve balance I believe many single parents reading this book will get remarried. (I also believe that many parents struggling in their marriage will be strengthened to stand for their marriage.) I believe they will apply the unity principles explained in this book and receive the emotional healing they need to have successful marriages. Many people who want to get remarried do not because they need emotional healing for their wounded souls. They have not learned the unity principles needed to receive emotional healing from the last marriage and from their parents.

God has put this book in your hands as one way for you to learn unity principles and receive emotional healing. During my parents' separation and following their divorce, I needed emotional healing. When my parents separated I longed for my Daddy. After my parents divorced, although I loved my father, I no longer longed for a daddy. Single parents, recognize that if your children have suffered through a divorce (the children also suffer), they will need emotional healing. Until they are healed, their fears could add to your fear of remarrying.

Single parents, God has prepared a father or a mother to partner with you for your children's sake. Don't give up! God has a balanced plan for your life.

God really does care about parents and their children (I Pet. 5:7). He cares about the relationship that parents have with their children.

The effort parents put into the relationship with their children says a lot about what kind of people they are. It says whether they are selfish parents or selfless parents.

Overcome Selfishness

A selfish parent is one who is impulsive. They may speak too quickly. They may spank too quickly. They may buy things too quickly. Many people think to be "selfish" is to only think about oneself. It does mean that, but it also means to not add value to the other people in your life.

A selfless parent is one who is cautious. They choose their words carefully. They use spanking as the last resort. They want to impart a sense of value for things in their child's life. Many people think to be "selfless" is to give all the time. It does mean to give, but it also means to train a child to view his parents as valuable.

Are you a selfish parent or a selfless parent? Are you seeing more selfishness in your children or more selflessness? Do they value you? One way you can determine if your children are valuing you is to ask them to give you something. It could be anything. If your child is very young, ask for a toy she is playing with. If your child is a teenager or an adult, ask for some money.

You could ask for a hug or a kiss. The idea behind this exercise is to see if you have taught your children to value you, not that you want something from your child. The Bible clearly says the parents are to lay up for the children (II Cor. 12:14). You just want to see if they value you. You want to see if they truly love you.

If your child is selfish, she won't give "it" to you. You may be able to coax it away from her, but that is not the point. You want her to give it to you. If your child is selfless, she will give it to you. (A side note: if you have a habit of asking your children for money, this exercise will not be necessary. If your children financially support you, they are showing that they value you.)

We have all had selfish ways from time to time and those times let us know that we are not walking in love. Parents and children can be selfish and not realize it, yet the parents have a responsibility to teach their children about love. We teach our children how to love by explanation and by comforting them. Our children will learn how to comfort others from how they were comforted. Do you still comfort your children? Please pray this prayer to ask God to help you love and comfort your children:

Heavenly Father, You are so good and Your mercy endures forever. I thank You that You care about me and my children. I am sorry for all the times that I have been selfish toward them. Please help me to be a selfless person and model self-lessness to my children. Please help me to truly love and comfort my children. I pray for the salvation of my children and that they will walk according to Your truth. I forgive them for acting selfishly. Please help my children to be self-less people and love You and me in Jesus' Name. Amen.

Many people participate in gardening as a rewarding hobby and gardeners know that if you till and fertilize the soil of your flower bed before planting, you have prepared a great foundation in which to raise your flowers. You can also expect wonderful, colorful blooms to rise up. In the same way, parenting is one of the most exciting and rewarding things in life you will ever do. If you prepare yourself spiritually, emotionally and physically, you will enjoy a wonderful relationship with your children and they will rise up to call you blessed (Prov. 31:28).

Firm Your Foundation

If the foundations are destroyed, what can the righteous do?
(Ps. 11:3)

The family is the foundation of any nation. Whenever I see the word *nation* in the Bible I think of families. (Amos 3:1-2) Whenever I hear songs about nations I think of families. We learn from the Old Testament that the nation of Israel is one big family (Gen. 12:2). The Bible is written as a record of how God deals with individual families and families of nations (Ezek. 36:23).

In the Old Testament, the families of Israel experienced the generational curse as well as the generational blessing (Deut. 11:26). Predominantly, the curse was on the families that did not follow God and the blessing was on the families that followed God.

As God dealt with the Old Testament families, so He deals with our families today. God deals with whole families and whole nations. You can see the curse on the families and nations that do not follow God, and you can see the blessing on the families and nations that follow God. God is not mocked; whatever you sow you will reap (Gal. 6:7). If you sow disobedience toward God, you will reap the curse. If you sow obedience toward God, you will reap the blessing.

The family is the institution designed by God to train its members in obedience. Teachers were not designed to do it, though they can enforce obedience. The government was not designed to do it, though it can enforce obedience. God said "You (parents) train up a child in the way that they should go and they will not depart from it." (author paraphrased Prov. 22:6)

Psalms 11:3 says, "If the foundations are destroyed, what can the righteous do?" The foundation of a family is the parents. A family can be made up of any combination of people. But the basic family structure is a father, a mother and a child or children. Parents are to teach their children to be obedient to God's Word. Still, parents need to obey God's Word in order to teach their children how to obey God's Word. When parents disobey God's Word they damage their children's foundations. They undermine their relationship with their children.

<u>Unwed Parents Damage Their Children's Foundation</u>

Many families today are headed up by unwed mothers. Unwed mothers are women and young girls who have participated in sex outside of marriage and have gotten pregnant. As I said in the Introduction, sex was created to produce children. Eve never said, "I will prove my love to Adam by sleeping with him." She said, "I have brought forth a man" (Gen. 4:1 NLT). Sex is to be pleasurable and it is to strengthen the marital bond, but the number one purpose of sex is to have children.

The problem for unwed mothers is not that they have birthed children. The problem is they have had sex outside of marriage. The problem is they have fornicated. Fornication is against God's Word. Children born to an unwed mother and an unwed father do not have parents who obey God's Word. Unwed parents damage their children's foundations. As I have said before, God intends for children to be born in a loving marital relationship.

God wants men and women to be virgins when they marry (I Cor. 6:13). A virgin is a man or a woman who has the self-control to wait to have sex until they get married. If people are not virgins when they marry, they start their relationship disobedient to God's Word. Therefore, when they marry they are not able to give themselves wholly to their mates. When you have sex with someone you give a part of your soul to that person. If you are not married to that person, you have an unrighteous place in her soul and she has an

46

unrighteous place in your soul. If you repent of fornication, there is no condemnation to you and God can cleanse you from all unrighteousness (Rom. 8:1).

When God forgives you He cleanses your heart from unrighteousness. God can really cleanse your heart from desiring to fornicate. God can cleanse your desires. He will cleanse you if you fully surrender yourself (spirit, soul and body) to Him.

You must agree to be cleansed. God will not do something out of your will. You must agree. As soon as He has your agreement to be cleansed, He cleanses you from all unrighteousness. He knows He has your agreement when you repent. Some people believe they have given God their agreement to be cleansed just by saying, "I'm sorry," but He doesn't have your agreement until you repent. Repentance means more than "I am sorry." It means, "I am sorry, what I did was wrong, and I won't do that anymore with God's help."

When you and I repent, not only are we cleansed, but we also are redeemed from the curse. Jesus redeemed, or freed us, from the curse with His sinless, holy blood (Gal. 3:13). His blood has the life of the Father in it. When we apply or plead Jesus' blood over our lives and our family members' lives, we are applying the life of the Father over us and them. Through Jesus' blood, we can have living and healthy relationships and not dying and unhealthy relationships. Through Jesus' blood we can be holy as He is holy (Lev. 11:44).

When we are holy we must let go of unholy relationships (II Cor. 6:14). Did you know God can take unholy people out of your soul? "How can He do that?" you may ask. He takes the pain of being with them out of your soul. He also takes the pleasure of being with them out of your soul. He breaks their unrighteous soul ties with you.

Unrighteous soul ties must be broken in order for you to truly receive the gift of righteousness. Many people have a hard time letting go of unrighteous relationships. God will not take those relationships away unless you surrender them to Him. But if you choose to keep them, unrighteous relationships keep the door open to the curse of disunity in your family.

Due to the high concentration of unwed mothers in low-income housing areas, we can easily see how unrighteous relationships keep the door open to the curse of disunity. In low-income housing areas marriage is not held in high honor. God's Word is not held in high honor. When God's Word is not held in high in honor, then the curse of disunity will operate in a family.

The curse of disunity is not limited to a poor family. However, poor relationships are limited to unrighteous relationships. Genesis 2:24 says, "For this cause shall a man leave his father and mother and be joined unto his wife and the two shall become one flesh." The two unite into one flesh. There must be unity in the marriage before there can be obedient children. Obedient parents produce obedient children. Disobedient parents produce disobedient children.

Parents Who Walk in Darkness Damage Their Children's Foundations

If you are an unwed parent, a divorced parent, or a married parent, your obedience will produce an avenue for obedience in your children. This book is a book of encouragement, not condemnation. God said he would keep his covenant of mercy with them that love Him and keep His commandments for a thousand generations (Ex. 20:6). When you turned from the darkness to the light, your children turned from a dark playing field to a lighted playing field. They now can see they have the choice to obey or disobey. It is in their hands. When the parents walk in darkness, the children almost have no choice. Without light, it is hard for children to see where they are going.

When the parents walk in darkness, the children almost always walk in darkness also (II Chron. 22:3-4). I say "almost" because there are exceptions. Many times in the Old Testament we see wicked kings who displeased God followed by their sons who pleased God. The children followed godly ways even though their parents didn't.

Ahaziah was a wicked king of Judah. After his death, his infant son, Joash, had to be hidden from Ahaziah's wicked mother, Athaliah. Athaliah wanted to reign and pursued her goal by killing all of her own son's sons. Athaliah attempted to kill all of her grandsons (II Chron. 22:10). Remember: the purpose of the curse of disunity is to destroy a family. And Athaliah would have accomplished her goal, except for the mercy of God. Joash's life was spared, but it was not due to the compassion of his grandmother. It was because of the compassion of his aunt. Ahaziah's sister, the wife of a godly priest, hid Joash from his grandmother. Joash was only saved because there were people around him who had compassion on him and were not afraid to stop the curse (II Chron. 22:10-11).

In Exodus 20:12 God says, "Honor your father and mother and it will be well with you." What if your parents were not the loving, nurturing or nourishing people toward you that they should have been? What if your parents damaged your foundation? What if your parents were abusive or like Athaliah and no matter what you did you could not please them? Mother Theresa has a famous poem about people. I have changed "people" to "parents" just so we remember who the people are we are talking about.

Parents are often unreasonable, illogical and self-centered;
Forgive them anyway.

If you are kind, your parents may accuse you
of selfish, ulterior motives;
Be kind anyway.

If you are successful, you will win
false *friendships with your parents and some true animosity from your parents*;
Succeed anyway.

If you are honest and frank, your parents may cheat you;
Be honest and frank anyway.

What you spend years building,
your parents could destroy overnight;
Build anyway.

If you find serenity and happiness,
your parents may be jealous;
Be happy anyway.

The good you do today, your parents will
forget tomorrow,
Do good anyway.

Give your parents the best you have, and
it may never be enough;
Give your parents the best you've got... anyway.

You see, in the final analysis, it is
between you and God,
It never was between you and your parents anyway.

If your parents abused you, in addition to reading this book, you may need to sit down and talk to someone, a trusted friend, a counselor, a pastor, who can help you overcome deep-rooted hurts. God does not want your hurts to remain. He wants you to have a healthy soul.

When you really forgive your parents for mistreating you, you can have a healthy soul and find a sense of peace you have never known. When you decide in the relationship with your parents (and really every relationship) to treat them with respect, in most cases, you will find that they will treat you with respect. You may say, "You don't know my parents." No, I may not know your specific parents, but I am a parent and I understand parenting. As a parent I understand that parents can make mistakes. As a parent I understand that parents can sin. As a parent I understand that our children can feel unloved, undernourished and not nurtured. I know these are reasons why children go away or disunite from their parents. However, as a child I also understand that God can heal our relationship with our parents. He said He would turn the hearts of the fathers back to their children and the hearts of the children back to their fathers (Mal. 4:6).

God can heal the places in your heart where your parents have hurt you, and God can heal the places in your parents' hearts where your grandparents hurt them. God is the God who heals you and He is the same God who heals your parents (Exod. 15:26). When your parents mistreated you, they were wrong. Still, they needed healing.

The curse of disunity is a generational curse. In order for the curse to operate in your life, there must be problems between you and your parents. You can't walk in disunity by yourself. Disunity is a people problem. It is a family problem.

Respect your father and mother and it will be well with you. Treat your father and mother right and it will be well with you. Do good towards your parents and it will be well with you. Take the pressure off your parents to make you happy and it will be well with you. God is the one backing the word that as you honor your father and mother, He will make it well with you.

Legalistic Parents Damage Their Children's Foundations

As parents and children we must stand on God's Word, however, parental legalism damages children's foundations. We cannot make our children love God. Zechariah 4:6 says, "It's not by power, nor by might, but by My Spirit." The Spirit of God causes people to love Him. We love Him because He first loved us (I Jn. 4:19). Second Timothy 3:1-5 says:

> But know this, that in the last days perilous times will come: For men will be lovers of themselves, lovers of money, boasters, proud, blasphemers, disobedient to parents, unthankful, unholy, unloving, unforgiving, slanderers, without self-control, brutal, despisers of good, traitors, head-strong, haughty, lovers of pleasure rather than lovers of God, having a form of godliness but denying its power. And from such people turn away!

Many children are prodigals because their parents have shown them the form of God, but their parents have denied the power of the love of God. Prodigals are children who have rebelled against the ungodly pressure their parents put on them to love God.

Many parents want their children to love God, yet they have not shown them a loving God. They have not shown them the love behind the Word of God. They have showed them the law. If you love and honor God and your children love and honor you, they will love and honor God. You cannot pressure your children to love God. They must make that decision on their own.

When you achieve unity of the faith with your children, you have achieved the ultimate in the realm of the generational blessing of unity. When we show our children God's love flowing through us, they will want God. If we show them dead and harsh religion, they will not see the loving God flowing through us. They will not want God. God is not a God in form, creed or doctrine only, but a God with loving power. He is the God of all power (Matt. 28:18). He has the power to help us walk in unity of the faith.

People can think they have God's power to walk in unity because they go to church. Just going to church will show that they have the form of being religious, but God sees your heart (I Sam. 16:7). He hears your complaints about your children. He hears your complaints about your parents. Many of you are not enjoying your relationship with all of your children or your parents because you have been complaining to God about them instead of thanking God for them. You may not be complaining outwardly, still God knows your thought patterns.

Just as we leave finger patterns or fingerprints on everything we touch, our actions display a pattern of what we have been thinking about. We live our lives according to thought patterns. This is why we should not try to be one person at work and another person at home. We may be able to put our best feet forward for a little while, but sooner or later our real selves will come out. Our patterns will appear. If we have a pattern of being impatient with the kids, the pattern of impatience will also show up with our subordinates at work. What we really think will appear.

God knows what we really think about everything. God knows who we are in every situation (Jer. 1:5). In every situation He knows whether we will honor Him or not. Say a situation comes up. Your children are being disruptive in the car. God is seeing and hearing your reactions in that situation. He is sensitive to your pattern of honor or dishonor. He is also sensitive to your children's pattern of honor or dishonor.

<u>Disobedient Children Damage Their Foundations</u>

What is the outcome for children who disobey God regarding their parents? Dishonor your father and mother and it will not be well with you. Disrespect your father and mother and it will not be well with you. Mistreat your father and mother and it will not be well with you. Make your parents sorrowful and it will not be well with you. Remember, God is the one backing up His Word.

The issue isn't parents versus children. The issue is authority. The issue is: Who is in authority? Have you ever heard the question, Which came first—the chicken or the egg? Well, who came first, the parents or the children? As we read through the genealogies in the Bible we can clearly see parents came first (Gen. 5:3). Parents are the foundational people in a child's life. Almost everything you learned about relationships you learned from your parents. If they taught you disunity, you are probably living in the curse right now. If they taught you unity, you are probably living in the blessing right now.

The blessing comes from God and the primary thing your parents were to teach you is how to stay in a unified relationship with God. God said He chose Abraham because he would command his children about Him (Gen. 18:19). God chose Abraham because he would teach his children how to relate to Him. When we come into a relationship with God through Jesus, we learn how to relate to God.

Jesus showed us how to relate to God through His example of laying His life down. He showed us that to relate to God we must lay our lives down. This requires obedience to the Word of God. Philippians 2:5-11 says:

Your attitude should be the same as that of Christ Jesus:

Who, being in very nature God, did not consider equality with God something to be grasped, but made himself nothing, taking the very nature of a servant, being made in human likeness. And being found in appearance as a man, he humbled himself and became obedient to death—even death on a cross! Therefore God exalted him to the highest place and gave him the name that is above every name, that at the name of Jesus every knee should bow, in heaven and on earth and under the earth, and every tongue confess that Jesus Christ is Lord, to the glory of God the Father.

The blessing of God will not fall on someone just because they want the blessing of God. The blessing of God is going to fall on someone because he humbled himself and became obedient (Phil 2:8). Honor your father and mother is God's commandment. A commandment is an instruction to obey. When my son was between three and four he started becoming more assertive. His two-year-old stage seemed mild compared to the three-year-old stage. He needed to learn what obedience meant.

I remember a time when he, my infant daughter and I were getting in the van to go somewhere and he didn't want to get in the van. Unfortunately, times like this were more frequent when he was three; however, they provided more opportunities for me to explain obedience to him.

So I said, "Andrew, obey." Then I pretended to be my daughter and said in a baby voice, "Mommy, what is 'obey'?" Then I answered in my maternal voice, "Obey means to do to whatever Mommy and Daddy tell you to do." Then I pretended to be an enlightened Anna and I squealed, "Oh…oh." At that point he understood what I meant and complied with my directions.

Although most of the time children know when they are disobeying their parents, they do not always know that they are damaging their foundation. Although they may expect unpleasant natural consequences to their actions, they are not always aware of the unpleasant spiritual consequences. Although they may try to hide to avoid unpleasant consequences, they hide in vain. The secret sins of the people in the body of Christ today are simply the results of children who hide in vain.

No one can hide from God. Numbers 32:23 says there is nothing that can be hidden from God. Proverbs 20:27 says God searches out the spirit of a man. Psalms 139:7 says there is no where we can go that His spirit can't find us. To some that may sound scary, but it is really good news. For even when we have been disobedient to our parents and disobedient to God's Word, His mercy can still find us.

Young children are taught this principle of "all-knowing" by their mother's ability to "see" everything they do. Children are so obvious when they are doing the wrong thing that it is not hard to see or hear what they are doing. Plus, as parents, we have trained our ears to hear our children. When my daughter was a baby I worked with the Infants in the Mother's Day Out program of my church. We could have up to twelve babies in the Infant program; still, I could hear my daughter's cry above any other baby's cry. God can see everything we do and He hears us when we call (Ps. 145:18). He is sensitive to our voice.

God knows you (Jer. 1:5). He knows you better than you know yourself. You may have said, "I would never do that," but you did. And God knew you would. He also knows that if you have not learned obedience, you are living on a faulty foundation and there is no shocking Him in what you will do. We may be shocked at our behavior sometimes, but God is not shocked. He can see our hearts (Ps. 44:21). He can see if we have a heart of unity or a heart of disunity.

A heart of unity comes from obeying parental authority. Parental authority is the root of all earthly authority. If a child will not obey his parents, he will not obey the educational authorities or the civic authorities. Isn't it sad to think of the people who are on death row simply because they would not obey authoritarian figures? It probably all started when they decided not to obey their parents.

God Will Judge

God is the ultimate authority of every authority and He is the parent of every parent. He wants parents to honor Him. He asks, "If I am a Father, where is my honor?" (Mal. 1:6). One day we will all stand before the judgment seat in heaven and if we are believers, our works (acts or deeds) of obedience will be judged in fire. First Corinthians 3:10-15 says:

According to the grace of God which is given unto me, as a wise masterbuilder, I have laid the foundation, and another buildeth thereon. But let every man take heed how he buildeth thereupon.

For other foundation can no man lay than that is laid, which is Jesus Christ.

Now if any man build upon this foundation gold, silver, precious stones, wood, hay, stubble;

Every man's work shall be made manifest: for the day shall declare it, because it shall be revealed by fire; and the fire shall try every man's work of what sort it is.

If any man's work abide which he hath built thereupon, he shall receive a reward.

If any man's work shall be burned, he shall suffer loss: but he himself shall be saved; yet so as by fire. (KJV)

God has laid a foundation for our children. As parents we are to build on the foundation of our children's hearts. God will judge our works. Did we obey God or not? God said to honor your father and mother. Are you doing it? Are your children doing it? Are your grandchildren doing it?

Damaged foundations discourage children from obeying God. If you, your children or grandchildren have damaged foundations, please pray this prayer:

Heavenly Father, I love you. Thank you for loving me. Thank you for my parents. I am sorry for participating in unrighteous relationships. I am sorry for disobeying Your Word. I am sorry for disobeying my parents and I am sorry for mistreating my children. I was wrong. Please forgive me. I forgive my parents for the times they have disappointed me. Help me to honor them. I forgive my children for the times they have disappointed me. Help me to teach my children and grandchildren Your loving ways. I want to honor you, Lord, in all that I do and say. I trust You to help me, in Jesus' Name. Amen.

Obey From the Heart

Do you consider yourself a submissive person? Most people know right away if they are submissive or not. Submission is the quality in the soul of a person that enables them to walk in obedience. When you submit to Authority, you will obey them. When you submit to your parents, you will obey them. When you submit to teachers, you will obey them. If you are a submitted person, you will obey the people in authority over you.

Some people believe they are submissive, but they are having a lot of problems in their lives. The lack of submission in your life will equal the effects of the curse manifesting in your life. Remember, a submitted person is a blessed person (Rev. 22:7).

Rebellious or Stubborn?

There are two roots that affect your ability to submit: rebellion and stubbornness. Rebellion, or aggressive behavior, is caused by a person refusing to declare that someone in authority is right. A rebellious adult or child will come right out and say, "No," "I am not going to," or "I won't." A rebellious person believes no one can tell them what to do. He believes he is right.

We all want to be right. We don't want to admit that someone else may be right, especially when it goes against what we think is right. We want to think they are wrong and we are right. Naturally speaking, there will be times when we are right and there will be times when we are wrong. We are human after all – fallible and certainly not all-knowing. We are not God. God is always right in every situation (Ps. 19:8). Every day in every way God's ways and His Word are always the right answer. We submit to His all-knowing self. We submit to His authority.

Stubbornness, or passive-aggressive behavior, is a quiet refusal to submit to godly authority. A stubborn adult or child will simply not do what she has been asked to do. She simply does not want to. She believes the person in authority is wrong. She believes the person in authority is mistaken.

God is the ultimate authority. He delegates His authority to people who represent Him in the earth. Parents are delegated representatives of God's authority.

There are times when we disagree with the leader. We should not respond rebelliously or stubbornly. If the leader or parent is not telling us to do something ungodly, we should submit. When we consistently reject godly authority, we set ourselves up for the curse to rule us.

When I was a Child...

The curse doesn't fall on a child for being a child. A child is going to test the boundaries his parents have set. There are times a child will talk back. There are times when a child will not obey. There are times when a wife or a subordinate will talk back to the person in authority. Those people are not necessarily under the curse. Anywhere there are leaders and subordinates there will be opportunities for rebellion and stubbornness to manifest.

God is not opposed to disagreements. He doesn't wither when there are relationship problems. He knows as people we are going to have to work things out. He can handle disagreements. We are not cursed if we commit random acts of disunity. We are not cursed for indiscriminate rebellion. We are not cursed for being haphazardly disrespectful. Although we want to avoid acting that way and we want to repent when we act that way, as human beings we are going to have times that we mishandle disagreements.

The curse does not come upon people simply because they disagree. The curse comes when our reactions to disagreements are consistently ungodly. The curse comes when we refuse to humble ourselves and handle disagreements in a godly way. The curse comes when we prolong disagreements. People who prolong disagreements are then said to have a disagreeable spirit, or a stubborn personality. Stubbornness is linked to iniquity. Iniquity is a sin practiced over and over.

A child may act rebelliously for a season. All children go through phases of testing parental authorities. However, they need to repent for disrespectful behavior. Children who do not repent grow into adults who still want to test the authorities. They have practiced rebellion.

God is opposed to stubborn and rebellious lifestyles. God told Saul, "For rebellion is as the sin of witchcraft and stubbornness is as iniquity and idolatry. Because thou hast rejected the Word of the Lord, He hath also rejected thee from being king" (I Sam. 15:23).

#1 Hindrance to Submission: Pride

Pride causes people to reject godly authority. God hates pride (Prov. 8:13). James 4:6 says God resists the proud and gives grace to the humble. God resists the proud. Many people think they can do whatever they want to do. Some people believe that is what it means to be free. That is not what being free means. Always doing whatever you want to do is prideful. There are many times throughout the day that a person has to obey laws, bosses, and spouses. No one can do whatever they want to do all the time.

There are times when we can do whatever we want to do. There are times when we don't need to see how what we do affects others. For example, when my children are at school and my husband is at work I can do whatever I want to do. Glory! Still, even during those times I have to stop doing whatever I want to do at some point and do something for someone else. At some point I have to pick my children up from school. At some point I have to cook dinner for my husband.

Submission is relegated to the time when we cannot do whatever we want to do and we must submit to what someone else wants to do. If people did whatever they wanted to do all the time, life would be chaotic. There wouldn't be any order. God is the God of order (I Cor. 14:40). He wants order in the home. Children are to obey, wives are to submit, and husbands are to lead under the headship of Christ.

Husbands are not under the headship of Christ alone. Children are also under the headship of Christ. Wives are also under the headship of Christ. Every Christian is to be under the headship of Christ; therefore, mutual submission will be necessary to maintain godly order (Eph. 5:21).

There will be times I tell my children what to do and there will be times when my children tell me what to do. Of course, asking each other to do something is much more preferable than directly telling each other what to do. Still, there are times when I submit to my children's wants, desires, and commands and there are more times that they submit to my wants, desires, and commands. In order for there to be unity, there must be times of mutual submission.

If I am putting some toys away in my son's room and he comes in and says, "No, Mommy. Put it over there." I can "obey" without there being any threat to my authority. It takes humility for a parent to listen to and carry out their child's demands. An extreme authoritarian parent will dare their child to tell him what to do. Authoritarian parents are the ones who pull out the "I am your parent and I said so" the most. Still, there will be many times (and I stress "many") that your child will simply need to obey you.

#2 Hindrance to Submission: Lying

Parents can hinder their children's ability to submit. When they tell their children to do things that are wrong, they are hindering their children. If a child is told to lie about his age so he can get into the theme park for a discounted price, that child could lie whenever he felt like it is convenient for him to lie.

People lie to gain an advantage. Yet lying does not give anyone an advantage. Lying cultivates mistrust (Col. 3:9). I believe there are many children of Christian parents who have not accepted Christ because they do not trust their parents' judgment. Why would they believe their parents who say God is good when the parents lie about other things?

Parents should be honest in order to train their children in submission. Parents should be honest if their children are to trust their parental judgments when they say, "Just do it."

Telling a child to lie isn't the only way to cultivate mistrust. Lack of parental follow through also cultivates mistrust. It is a form of lying. If we say we are going to do something, we should follow through with our word. We want to avoid lying to our children in order that they can grow up to be trusting people.

Trusting people exude confidence in their relationships. They have less fear in developing friendships. If our children are trusting people, they will exude confidence, have less fear, and have healthy souls. If our children are trusting people they will have no problem trusting God (Prov. 18:24).

Trusting people can believe that God is not a man that He should lie or the son of man that He should repent (Num. 23:19). Trusting people believe that God doesn't lie (Ps. 89:35). Most people will not submit to people they don't trust. Of the people who do not submit to God, most of them will not submit to God because they don't trust Him. When we believe that God is trustworthy we do not struggle to walk by faith. We do not struggle with His instructions. We trust God.

#3 Hindrance to Submission: Wanting Control

We can trust that Jesus has already redeemed us from the curse (Gal. 3:13). When He died and went to hell He took the keys of hell, death and the grave from the devil. Jesus took the keys of all death. Death no longer rules over us. There are many relationships that die because the people involved had a disagreement. Your relationships do not have to die because you disagree.

Most disagreements are over who is in control. Who is in control? God is the ultimate person who is in control. Still He has delegated His authority in the earth. If you do not honor godly authority in your life, you will not be able to walk freely in your authority. Your ability to use your authority and command the curse off of your life will equal your ability to submit to godly authority. You will not have the power to break the curse off of your life if you are a disobedient person. If you do not have the power to obey, you will not have the power to break the curse. If you do not submit to godly authority, the devil will not flee from you (Jas. 4:7).

All authority comes from God (Rom. 13:1). Because authority is a godly principle, people who are in authority are anointed by God to tell others what to do. Most people are too casual with authority figures. Therefore, they do not give them the respect that they deserve. They do not submit to them easily.

Jesus told Pilate, who had the authority to crucify Him, that he would have no power over Him, except that it was given to him by God (Jn. 19:11). Jesus recognized Pilate's position and authority, but He was not afraid of Pilate. He recognized that all authority comes from God.

One day a centurion sent a message asking Jesus to come and heal his servant of an illness. As Jesus was coming, the centurion sent another message saying, author paraphrased, "I understand authority. Speak the Word only and my servant will be healed." Because that centurion, who was not a Jewish person, exemplified the fact that he understood authority, Jesus said he had great faith (Matt. 8:5-13).

I make the distinction that the centurion was not a Jewish person because in Jesus' day only the Jews thought they had faith in God. Yet here was a person who understood authority that Jesus said had great faith. Some people think because they go to church a lot that they have great faith. It is only when you can submit to godly authority figures that you display that you have great faith in God (I Pet. 2:13-15).

Key #1 to Submission: Faith

If our child is misbehaving and we simply do not have time to explain every detail of our instructions, she simply will need to obey. She will need to obey out of blind faith. Every instruction, however, will not always need to be obeyed out of blind faith. We can tell our children why we want them to do something and how we want it done. We can give them detailed instructions. However, our not giving them detailed instructions does not excuse them from obeying. If I tell my son to clean his room, he needs to clean his room. If I tell him to pick up his socks, put away his toys and make up his bed, I give him the details of what I want done. Yet the bottom line is I want him to clean his room (and there might be a surprise awaiting his obedience).

Blind faith is necessary in our Christian walk as well as our natural walk of life. There will be times (many times) that God wants us to do something. There will be many times that He wants us to obey and we simply need to obey Him (Deut. 6:3; I Jn. 5:3). Blind faith with God occurs when we only know God said do it and we do it. We do not have the specifics. We don't always know the why. As Dr. Charles Stanley has said on many of his TV broadcasts, "Obey God and leave the consequences to Him."

Abraham's faith is our classic example of blind faith. God told him to go to a mountain. Abraham went to the mountain. God told him to sacrifice his son. Abraham lifted up the knife. The angel called to him, "Do not slay Isaac." A ram was caught in the thicket (Gen. 22:1-10). Abraham did not know when he lifted his knife that a ram was caught in the thicket. He trusted God so much that he would do anything He said. Abraham was a submitted man.

We would like for God to give us every detail of our lives for the next twenty years, but He doesn't do that. He expects us to trust Him. He expects us to live by faith. Sometimes He leads us one step at a time; more often though, God will reveal more of His plans to us when we spend time in fellowship with Him. In Jeremiah 33:3 God says, "Call to me and I will answer you and tell you great and unsearchable things you do not know." When we spend time in prayer, God will oftentimes give us the when, where, why and how details of His instructions.

If we spend time in prayer like Jesus did, we will receive the information that we need. Jesus spent a lot of time in prayer (Matt. 14:23; Mk. 6:46; Luke 6:12). And at no time was Jesus caught off guard. God showed Him the plan. God showed Him the details of the plan. Jesus knew where the colt was that He was to ride into Jerusalem (Mk. 11:2-7). He knew where He and the disciples were to eat the Last Supper (Matt. 26:17-19). He knew when He was to die (Jn. 12:23-27).

Jesus did not obey out of blind faith. He obeyed with the full knowledge of the what, the when, the where and the why. Hebrews 12:2 says for the joy set before Him He endured the cross, despising the shame. Jesus knew that after He obeyed He would sit at the right hand of the Father, full of power and glory (I Pet. 3:22). He knew there was a reward coming for His obedience.

There is a reward for your obedience (Matt. 16:27). There is a reward for living by faith. Living by faith does not mean that you don't know what is going to happen next. Living by faith means you are going to obey no matter what happens next. Abraham did not have all the details of why he was to sacrifice his only son when God told him to do it. Yet he was willing to do it knowing that if he sacrificed Isaac God would raise him back to life (Heb. 11:17-19).

Many people say, "I am living by faith." Some people say this to mean 'I am living, but I don't know what is going to happen next.' The truth is, while not knowing the exact details of what is going to happen next, the person living by faith will know what is going to happen next. Living by faith means you know that God is going to take care of you (Phil. 4:19). Living by faith means you know that God is going to provide (Gal. 3:9). The specifics may not be clear, but the outcome is clear. We obey God and leave the consequences to Him.

You may be reading this book by faith. Your family may have many disunity problems. You may not know how God is going to fix the problems. You may not know when He is going to fix the problems. Nevertheless, if you will apply the principles of this book by faith, you can trust God to bring His Word to pass. You can trust God that if you honor your father and mother, it will be well with you. God has a good plan for your life. You must believe it. You must trust God.

The just shall live by faith (Rom. 1:17; Gal. 3:11). It will take faith to consistently submit to godly authority. It will take your believing in the goodness of God to trust godly authority. When you reject authority on a consistent basis you oppose God. When you reject authority God opposes you. If you and God are not on the same side, your ability to break the generational curse off of your life will be impossible (Mark 9:23).

Key #2 to Submission: Forgiveness

There is only one reason I believe people will not submit to godly authority. They have not learned forgiveness. They have been rejected. They have not been nourished and nurtured. They have lost respect for that authority figure. You will not submit to someone whom you have not forgiven. Because all human authority is fallible

– parents make mistakes, husbands mess up, teachers accuse the wrong child – in order to submit, you must forgive.

All of us are wrong sometimes and we can usually recognize when other people are wrong. However, we are not called to be faultfinders, but gapstanders (Prov. 10:11). We are not called to be faultfinders, but submitted. Submission, often disguised as love, believes the best about the person who is in authority over us. You can still have a submissive attitude even when the person in authority is wrong. God's Word shows us it can be done.

Look at the life of Saul and David. When God chose David to be king of Israel, Saul was still the king. Saul became intensely jealous of David. He tried to literally and overtly kill David, but David would not retaliate. Although David "went away", he continued to respect Saul. He called him "father" (I Sam. 24:1-22).

God has given us the example of submission for the times when the person in authority is wrong. Even though the person in authority may be trying to hurt you, you can still treat her respectfully. In the case of abuse, you need to seek counsel and separate yourself and your children from the person abusing you or your children. David separated himself from Saul. Yet he continued to speak of Saul respectful manner, even though he no longer obeyed him. Your speech testifies whether you are honoring the person in authority or not. Matthew 12:34 says that out of the abundance of the heart the mouth will speak.

When a person does not have a submissive attitude toward their parents they will have very negative things to say about them. Name calling, put downs, slander will all be a part of a person's speech that dishonors their parents. Unforgiveness creates bitterness in your soul, not your parents'. Even though you have been mistreated, to a certain degree everyone has, God has not changed His mind about submission to authority (Rom. 13:2). He knows that if you will not submit to people whom you can see, you will not submit to Him whom you cannot see.

Jesus said if you will not forgive, you will not be forgiven (Matt. 6:14). Forgiving is just as a much as a commandment as "honor your father and mother" (Ex. 20:12). Forgiving is just as much a part of God's Word as "thou shalt not steal" (Ex. 20:15). If you do not obey the Word of God, you are on the opposite end of the blessing. If you do not obey the Word of God, you give access to the curse to enter your life.

Key #3 to Submission: Surrender to God

God is a good God. Oral Roberts was the person who popularized that phrase. God is a good God (Ps. 25:8). Many times because something 'bad' has happened to them people doubt or don't trust in the goodness of God. Bad things happening do not negate the fact that God is good. Bad things happening are the result of the curse being loosed on the earth through disobedience.

Psalm 23 is a picture of the relationship that God wants to have with us (I have changed the wording to reflect God's point of view):

> I am your shepherd; You shall not want.
> I make you to lie down in green pastures: I lead you beside the still waters.
> I restore your soul: I lead you in the paths of righteousness for My name's sake.
> Yea, though you walk through the valley of the shadow of death, you will fear no evil: for I am with you; it is My rod and My staff that comforts you.
> I prepare a table before you in the presence of your enemies: I anoint your head with oil; Your cup runs over.
> Surely goodness and mercy shall follow you all the days of your life: and you *will dwell in My house for ever.*

When we think of the Lord as our Shepherd we must think of ourselves as the sheep. Sheep follow the shepherd. We have to follow the Shepherd. We have to lay down where He tells us to lay down. We have to walk where He tells us to walk. We have to allow Him to lead us. When we submit to Him, goodness and mercy will follow us all the days of our lives. Submissive behavior sets people up to be blessed. Disobedient behavior sets people up to be cursed.

There are times when a person is breaking the curse that bad things seem to happen. When you are breaking the curse, you are breaking from the kingdom of darkness to the kingdom of the light (Col. 1:13). The devil will not be happy that you are breaking from his kingdom. He likes the fact that your relationships are not healthy.

David was a blessed man, yet Saul pursued him as though he was cursed (I Sam. 16:13). David was to set up a new kingdom. Saul's kingdom was passing away, but he would not allow it to pass away without trying to destroy David. David had opportunities when he could have destroyed Saul (I Sam. 24:11, 26:7). He could have gotten so angry at Saul that he could have killed Saul.

Yet David proved that he was blessed and did not curse Saul. When you are cursed, you curse. You may even cuss. David never cursed Saul. He never said, "This is my kingdom. Give it to me!" He recognized that as long as Saul lived God had anointed Saul to be the leader over Israel (I Sam. 24:6). David recognized that God backs leaders. David proved why he was a man after God's own heart. He stayed submitted to the will of God even during times of adverse treatment by a person in authority (Acts 13:22).

Numbers 12:3 says Moses was the meekest man on earth. What makes a person meek? They do not strike back at a person even though that person has hurt them. Many times Moses prayed for the Israelites when they murmured against him (Ex. 16:7; 17:4). Jesus said, "If a person hits you on the left cheek turn the other cheek" (Matt. 5:39). Most people are armed and ready to protect themselves. Many people are ready to let you have it if you cross them. God said He would protect you (Ps. 12:5-6). You can believe Him to protect you. You can believe Him when you surrender your life to Him.

Godly Leaders Are Submitted People

Your level of submission to God and His ways, which is in His Word, will determine what kind of leader you will be. Promotion comes to everyone. Everyone will have the opportunity to be a leader. Parents generally beget parents. As a parent, you must realize your children will be leaders one day – of your grandchildren, of a corporation, of a ministry, of a department, or of a shift.

God has destined our children to be leaders. They are to be the head and not the tail, above and not beneath, over and not under (Deut. 28:13). The generational curse is that our children will not rise to be godly leaders. You as the parent are to teach your child how to be a godly leader. If you were an unwed mother, and your daughter becomes an unwed mother, your child did not learn godly leadership from you. She is a leader but not a godly leader. Paul outlines traits of a godly leader for Timothy. Although Paul is talking to Timothy about church leadership, these principles can be applied in any area for effective leadership.

> Here is a worthy saying: If anyone sets his heart on being an overseer, he desires a noble task.
>
> Now the overseer must be above reproach, the husband of one wife (or wife of one husband), temperate, self-controlled, respectable, hospitable, able to teach, not given to drunkenness, not violent but gentle, not quarrelsome, not a lover of money.
>
> **He must manage his own family well and see that his children obey him with proper respect.**
>
> **(If anyone does not know how to manage his own family, how can he take care of God's church?)** (I Tim. 3:1-5)

The character principle I want to emphasize is a married or single leader must manage his family well and see that his children obey him with proper respect. Paul is saying, "If anyone does not know how to manage his own family, how can he be a godly leader?"

The family should be the background check for leadership. When a family is in disunity there are reasons that should not be ignored. A teenager becomes an unwed parent for a reason. In most cases teenagers want to lead or grow up too fast because of the faulty leadership they see at home. The leadership isn't faulty because of imperfect parents. There are no perfect parents. The leadership is faulty because they have not trained their children to submit to them. I once heard this statement: "A leader isn't a leader if no one is following. He is simply taking a walk." Parents are to lead their teenagers. Parents encourage their teenagers to follow by loving, nurturing and nourishing them.

Teenagers do not make good leaders until they have learned to submit to their parents. No one is a good leader if they do not have a good attitude towards their parents. A good leader is a submissive person. A good leader will love, nourish and nurture the people subordinate to him.

In a situation where you are a grandparent standing against the curse of disunity, your help will be greatly needed to prevent the curse from manifesting itself in your grandchild. Help your grandchild honor his father and mother. Help your grandchild submit. Help your grandchild forgive his parents. Love, nourish and nurture your children and grandchildren.

Submission: A Daily Decision

There is a fork in the road for every child. Go left to disobey. Go right to obey. Parents, grandparents, teachers, friends, aunts, and uncles need to be in place to always help that child choose to go right.

We never know when a child's act of disobedience will change the entire direction of her life. There was a case a few years ago of a pudgy twelve-year-old boy who had killed a four- or five-year-old little girl. He had performed a fatal wrestling move on her. It was an accidental death. It was tragic. I wonder, though, how many times that little boy had been told not to play rough with that little girl. It was a life-changing moment. That little boy went to prison. Later he was moved to a juvenile detention center. The little girl went to heaven.

A life-changing moment can occur without any warning. We have to be aware of the forks in the road. Throughout a child's life, a fork will appear before her. A fork indicates a decision is needed to be made to go this way or that way. Left or right. Towards the devil or towards God.

Children make decisions every day, but only a few of those will be life-changing. There are good life-changing decisions, for example, when a child accepts Christ, and there are bad life-changing decisions, like when a child first chooses to drink an alcoholic beverage. We don't know when a child will make a life-changing decision. However, we want to prepare him to make right decisions every time.

Children are like computers. They gather information on a daily basis. The information they gather determines which direction they will go when the fork appears. When a child decides to do something disastrous he did not wake up one day and decide to destroy his life. Simply, more destructive information piled up in his mind than constructive. That child simply took more pleasure in disobeying than in obeying. That child took more pleasure in rebelling than submitting.

Submission Can Be Fun

If parents will be creative in thinking of fun activities for their children to do, their children will have positive experiences with submission. If parents will play with their children, the children will be able to appreciate submitting to their parents' ideas rather than to dread submitting to their rules and regulations. Children learn by playing. Yes, they can hear and obey, yet if you make life a team effort, they will learn to submit. Everything cannot be a playful time; nevertheless, children need play-filled times. Although they may be playing, they are still learning. Never underestimate the power of play.

Children are not only nurtured by learning to submit to the rules of the game, children and adults benefit from playing. Children's souls feel free when they are playing. Adults feel refreshed after playing. Life is not all work.

Life is not all play either; therefore, it is a good idea to have a transition from playtime to real life time for children. When my son was very young, I learned he was happier if he knew the fun time was coming to end as opposed to ending the fun time abruptly. I would say, "In 15 minutes we are leaving the park." I would continue to count down, "You have 10 minutes...5 minutes. Okay, let's go." I would signal him to let him know playtime was coming to an end and I avoided him having a melt down because he was unprepared to stop playing. He could more easily submit to me when it was time to go if he was prepared for change.

I know as an adult I like to have a transition. If I go on a trip, I don't want to come back to a normal routine right away. I want to ease back into it. My husband likes to have a transition from work to home. His work life is so different from his home life. He doesn't work around children. He doesn't work in a homey atmosphere. He needs time to get his mind back on family life. Transition time is necessary to prepare us for change. It establishes a new direction in our minds. It moves us from where we have been to where we are going.

God is Simple

There are simple things we can do to maintain unity in our families. As we submit to God, we will be able to do things His way to achieve family unity. God put our families together. He knows how they should work. His ways are simple ways.

Repent From the Heart

The way to truly break the cycle of disunity is by repenting. When did you open the door of disunity? Were you a child or a teenager? Have you done things that you would never want your parents to know about? We have all done things we would not want our parents to know about and these things are things we need to repent for. We need to wipe the slate clean with our parents. We need to close the door of disunity where it was first opened.

Repent to Your Parents

We close the door of disunity by repenting to our parents for doing things we should not have done to them and against them. Though there are probably some specific things you may want to repent to your parents about, repentance does not mean to tell your parents everything you ever did that you knew you should not have done. Repentance means to turn around. Say you are going east on the freeway for a long trip. Then you notice a sign saying you are going west. You don't want to go west. You want to go east. So you do what? You get off the highway going west and get back on the highway going east.

When we repent to our parents we get off the highway of disunity, we turnaround and get back on the highway of unity. When we repent to our parents, we stop going away from our parents and we start going with our parents. When we repent to our parents, we can now have a better, more fulfilled relationship with them.

Repent to God

Saying "I'm sorry, I was wrong and I won't do it again" is a powerful medium to get family relationships back on the right path. Saying "I'm sorry, I was wrong and I won't do it again" is a powerful medium to get you back on the right path with God. Many people believe because they grew up going to church, they were sprinkled in baptism as a baby, or their parents go to church that they are on the right path with God. They believe they are children of God or Christians because of outward "things." A Christian is simply a person who follows Christ.

A Christian is someone who does what Jesus would do. In order to do what Jesus would do, we must believe that He is the Son of God (Matt. 17:5). In order to do what Jesus would do, we must accept Him as our Lord and Savior. When we do that we become everything He is. First John 4:17 says as He is, so are we in this life.

Jesus is the Son of God and the Son of Man. When He lived on earth, He was fully God and fully man. Many people accept the deity of Christ without accepting the humanity of Christ, or they accept that Jesus was human, but not divine. The divine side of Him connected Him to God. The human side of Him connected Him to people.

Jesus' life on earth was always natural and spiritual. When He died on the cross and His human blood was poured out, it was holy blood. He poured it out in obedience to God and He poured it out for people. He kept His relationship right with God and people so that you and I could keep our relationship right with God and people. Jesus kept His relationship right with His Father so that you and I could keep our relationship right with our parents (Jn. 17:22).

When Jesus comes into our hearts God becomes our Father (Rom. 8:17). There are two ways to determine if God is really your Father. The first way is by the blood test. Have you been washed in the blood? Have you accepted that Jesus died for your sins and through His blood you have forgiveness of your sins? If you have, the Spirit inside of you will bear witness that you are a child of God (Rom. 8:16).

The second way to determine if you are a child of God is once you have accepted Jesus as your Savior, you want to learn His ways (Matt. 11:29). You want your children to know His ways. You want strangers to know His ways.

Walk in His Ways

God suffered so much to show you He loves you. He also suffered that you might know His ways. He suffered so that you might know Him and His ways of relating to others. When you have God's Spirit inside of you, you will relate to others the way God would relate to them. Your personality will reflect His Spirit. Your personality will reflect the fruit of the Spirit. The fruit of the Spirit is love, joy, peace, patience, kindness, goodness, gentleness, faithfulness, and self control (Gal. 5:22).

The only way you will be able to overcome the curse of disunity is that you walk in the Spirit. The only way you will be able to overcome the curse of disunity is that you become a loving, joyful, peaceful, patient, kind, good, gentle, faithful and self-controlled person for a long period of time. You may say, "I can be all of that for a certain period of time," but we need to be all of that for a long period of time. Galatians 5:16 says for us to walk in the Spirit and we will not gratify the lusts of the flesh.

The flesh in this instance is not the flesh and blood of our bodies. The flesh in this instance is old sinful ways of behavior (Rom. 8:4). We are to crucify the flesh. We are not to make excuses for our behavior. We are not to blame our parents for our behavior. We are to accept responsibility for what we have done, repent and do those things no more (Jn. 8:11).

When we deny the flesh we kill or overcome the sin nature. When we deny our flesh we will sin no more. The sin nature is the part of us that likes to sin. It is the part of us that likes to be disobedient to God.

The Spirit inside of us is the part of us that likes to be obedient to God. The question is, "Have you died?" Have you died to sin? Are you alive to righteousness? (I Pet. 2:24). When you give in to sin often, you develop a stronghold in your mind. Those automatic "mean" reactions are the effect of a stronghold in your mind. The "but I can't help it" mentality is the effect of a stronghold in your mind.

Be Influenced by God

A stronghold is a negative mindset. It is a cursed way of thinking. A stronghold is made of images that come up from your "memory bank" of all the times you felt mistreated by someone in authority over you and you resisted them. Your mind has stored in its memory bank all the times you resisted someone who was in authority over you – starting with your parents. Again, when we repent of our sins, God will cleanse our memories. Through God we pull down strongholds and cast down vain imaginations (II Cor. 10:4-5).

Vain imaginations are not from God. Some people say they don't know whether they are being influenced by what God wants, by what the devil wants, or by what they want. The only way to know is to examine the result, or fruit, of what you did. Godly wisdom is known by all her children (Matt. 11:19). If the fruit is something that praises and glorifies God, then God influenced your actions. If the fruit is something that dishonors God's Word, then you know the devil influenced your actions. If the fruit is something that twists the Word of God, then you know you influenced yourself.

To say, "I honor my father and mother," God influenced you to say that. That is God's Word; therefore He influenced you. To say, "I will not honor my father and mother," the devil influenced you. The devil hates the things of God. He strongly opposes everything in your life like God. To say, "I honor my father and mother" in front of them, but behind their backs malign their character is something you decided to do.

Sometimes when we examine the fruit of our behavior, we are shocked to see how much of what we do is directly influenced by the devil and how much of what we do is directly influenced by ourselves. When we directly resist the Word of God the devil has influenced us. He wants us to worship him. When we partially obey God, we have twisted the Word of God. The devil gets just as much delight from you twisting the Word of God as he would if you out rightly declared him as lord. When we fight the sinful nature, we are fighting the devil's desire to be lord of our lives and we are fighting our desire to be lord of ourselves.

We Are More Than Conquerors

Paul said that we are more than conquerors through Christ (Rom. 8:37). What is it that we are conquerors over? Many Christians want victory over the devil. We have it. When Jesus went down into hell, he triumphed over death, hell and the grave. Yet because many

75

people do not have victory over self, they are unable to maintain victory over the works of the devil. Just as much as we have to stand our ground against evil, we have to stand our guard against our flesh. Paul says he buffets his body so that after he has taught others he himself will not be a cast away (I Cor. 9:27).

Notice he didn't say he buffeted the devil with many words. He didn't say he rebuked the devil all day long. Paul said he buffeted his own body. *Buffet* means to struggle or force a way by struggling. Paul struggled against his own self. In Roman 7:24 he declares, "O, wretched man, that I am. Who can deliver me from this body of death? Thanks be unto God who causes me to triumph." Jesus causes us to triumph over the sinful nature.

You can't blame your bad attitude on the devil. You should take responsibility for your bad attitude. You can change your attitude any time you want to. When David was sad or mad, he reminded himself to bless the Lord (Ps. 103:1). When you take your eyes off of you and put them onto the Lord, the Lord will help you overcome a bad attitude or self-pity.

Self-pity is not from the devil. Self-pity is another way we decide to rule ourselves. Galatians 5:19-21 lists the fruit of the sinful nature. Among that fruit is selfish ambition, fits of rage, and dissension (Gal. 5:20). These three fruit of the sinful nature are so common that we tend to overlook, or ignore, them. What we ignore we don't conquer. When we conquer these three fruits I believe we conquer the curse of disunity in our families.

Godly Sorrow Changes Everything

You conquer your flesh by repenting of your sins. As I have already mentioned, when you repent of your sins you are not just sorry. When you repent you are purposing in your heart not to do that wrong thing again. When you repent God cleanses your heart (I Jn. 1:9). God knows when you have really repented or when you just said you were sorry. He can actually see your heart.

In First Samuel 15, Israel's first king, Saul, disobeyed the word of the Lord and he said he was sorry. As the leader, he was to make sure everything of the Amalekites was destroyed. He didn't.

Everything was not destroyed. Saul said he was sorry, but God could see Saul's heart. God could see Saul was not sorry for disobeying Him. God could see that Saul only said he was sorry, but he was not actually sorry. God knows when you are really sorry. Again, He can see your heart.

He can see the pattern of your heart. Until you repent of sin, a dishonorable heart will lead you farther and farther away from God. In the case of Saul, one day he sought the advice of a witch because he couldn't hear from God anymore (I Samuel 28). Israel's second king, David, also disobeyed God. David committed adultery and murder. Big sins, huh? Yet when he repented, he was truly sorry; therefore God forgave him (Ps. 51). David was a man after God's own heart (Acts 13:22).

When we have heartfelt repentance we are not looking for opportunities to dishonor our parents. When we have heartfelt repentance God will forgive us. God will forgive us for the sins we committed against our parents and He will also forgive us of sins we have committed against our children. God is watching how we treat our children. He is watching to see if we are parenting His way or in a confusing, selfish or angry way.

God Will Help Us

Behavior is the difference between a Christian parent and a non-Christian parent. A Christian parent's behavior reflects the fruit of the Spirit, and a non-Christian parent's behavior will reflect the fruit of the sinful nature. One behavior leads to eternal life for them and their children. The other leads to eternal damnation for them and their children.

There are some good parents who are not Christian. However, only a Christian can display the fruit of the Spirit and have the Spirit of God in them to help them parent their children. Non-Christian parents do not have access to the Spirit of God and can only depend on themselves and the devil's influence to parent their children.

In order for God's Spirit to help us walk in unity with our family members, we must maintain our relationship with the Lord. Sin should not be taken lightly, and especially as Christian parents, we must understand that our behavior affects a generation. Our children are depending on us to show them how to live for Christ. Our children are depending on us to live rightly with the Lord and with them. Sin dims our view of everything, even our responsibility to our children (I Jn. 2:11).

When we repent of our sins our souls get restored (Ps. 23:3). Our view gets clearer (Prov. 4:18). Then we can understand how to relate to God and others. We don't have to flounder around in our relationships with our children and others.

God can uncomplicate our relationships. Jesus came to earth to restore us to God and to restore our ability to relate well to others. Jesus has done His part. Now we must examine our ways to see if we are doing our part (II Cor. 13:5).

Examine Your Ways

Communion is a time instituted by Jesus at the Last Supper for us to examine our ways. It is a time to remember that Jesus' body was broken and His blood was poured out for us (I Cor. 11:23-25). We take the bread and juice and examine how we are living our lives in the light of what Jesus has done. It's a time for us to remember that we have a new covenant.

Jesus is the Mediator of the new covenant. Paul said many Christians sleep because they devalued the new covenant (I Cor. 11:30). When he says "sleep," he means they died untimely deaths. He says people devalue the new covenant by not repenting of their sins and allowing the blood of Jesus to cleanse them from all unrighteousness. In order to truly value the covenant with Jesus, we must examine our hearts, repent of our sins and allow His blood to cleanse us.

Communion isn't the only time that you should repent of your sins Every time you sin in thought, word or deed you should repent. Yet communion is a time when you should specifically repent of your sins. At my home church, we partake of communion during our Wednesday night services. There are times before the service I am reminded of a bad attitude. I see that my heart is not right. So I humble myself, repent and trust that the blood of Jesus cleanses my heart from sin. Then I can go to church with a clear conscience.

At communion if the pastor discusses the issue I had already dealt with, I can be at peace knowing I have already dealt with that issue. If I had not listened to God when He wanted to deal with me earlier that day, that night I would not have been ready to partake of communion until I repented.

Repentance was instituted as a way to keep our hearts rightly connected to God. Spending time with God is also a way to keep us rightly connected to God. We find in the scriptures that Jesus went away to a solitary place to pray and just to be with God (Luke 5:16). I believe by spending time with God, Jesus was also able to stay rightly-related with people. I believe by my spending time with God I will also be able to stay rightly-related with people.

Everything that Christ could do in relationships I can do (Phil. 4:13). I can stay rightly-related to God and to my parents. I can stay rightly-related to God and my spouse. I can stay rightly-related to God and my children. Maintaining my relationships with people is just as spiritual as maintaining my relationship with God. And to do it, Jesus must increase and I must decrease (Jn. 3:30).

We all must decrease the sinful nature and increase the fruit of the Spirit to stay rightly-related with others and God (Rom. 8:6). On one occasion I wanted some furniture, but I had a lot of clutter in the space that I wanted the furniture to fill. The Lord told me to remove the clutter so that I would have room for the new furniture. So many of us want unity in our families, yet the area in our hearts is cluttered with anger, selfishness and rejection. We must decrease our own ways in order to receive God's ways. We must make room for not just unity, but for the Unifier. God is the One who brings unity to a family (Ps. 68:6).

Here is a prayer of repentance:

Lord, here is my heart. I invite You to live in me. I am sorry for my sins. I am sorry for disrespecting my parents. I am sorry for disobeying You. Help me to walk in Your ways. Help me to walk in the fruit of Your spirit. I pull down strong-

holds and vain imaginations that have prevented me from walking in your truth. I can do all things through Christ who strengthens me. Father, I will walk in Your truth and light. Thank You for loving me so much. Amen.

This is a turning point in your life on the path of unity and generational blessing. Now would be a good time to take communion. Simply get a piece of bread and a little juice. It would be a good idea to read over First Corinthians 11:23-25 as you take communion.

God has a plan for your children. The generational curse of disunity hinders that plan from coming to pass. God's plan is that your family work together as one team, one man (Jdg. 20:1). The following section details the concepts that prevent your family from being in one accord. As you continue reading this book, allow the Spirit of God to open the eyes of your understanding.

Section Two

And You shall be called a repairer of the breach....
(Isa. 58:12)

Exposing the Generational Curse

This book is about your having the ability to break the generational curse of disunity. The curse of disunity causes a breach in your family. You shall be called to repair the breach (Isa. 58:12). You shall spread the healing balm of the blessing of unity over your family. First, however, you must understand how your family was broken. In the last chapter I used the unwed grandmother and mother as an example of the generational curse of disunity. In this section I want to discuss how the curse originated and how it continues generation after generation.

The first account of disunity is given in Genesis 3:1-19. There we learn that Satan lied to Eve and told her not to honor God's Word. He told her she could "eat of the tree of the knowledge of good and evil." Eve believed the serpent and ate of the tree. Her behavior separated herself from God. After Adam had also eaten some of the fruit, the curse of disunity came on mankind. Consequently, their decision to sin, to dishonor God, allowed Satan to deceive people to dishonor God and put the curse of disunity in operation in their families.

The curse of disunity has been at work since the decision was made to dishonor God's Word. Getting people to dishonor God is the oldest trick that the devil plays on people. He uses deception and fear to entice people to dishonor God. We see people, children and adults, dishonoring God's Word and walking in fear. God's Word is the final authority (Ps. 19:7). When people believe Satan's lie they give in to disobedience, which causes a break in the unity between God and man. Disobedience to God's Word is what opens the door for a curse to manifest in the lives of people.

My definition of a curse is the devil's destructive plan to devalue a person by means of negative experiences in life until she is destroyed (Jn. 10:10). God intends for life to be good, but the devil intends for life to be hard (Rom. 6:23). God intends for His children to have free access to Him, but disobedience puts a chasm between God and man (Matt. 9:13). God intends for life to be simple, but disobedience complicates life (Ps. 1:1-3).

The Curse

God's explanation of the curse is found in Deuteronomy 28:15-68. Pay special attention to the parts about the family relationship.

15 However, if you do not obey the Lord your God and do not carefully follow all His commands and decrees I am giving you today, all these curses will come upon you and overtake you:

16 You will be cursed in the city and cursed in the country.

17 Your basket and your kneading trough will be cursed.

18 **The fruit of your womb will be cursed** and the crops of your land, and the calves of your herds and the lambs of your flocks.

19 You will be cursed when you come in and cursed when you go out.

20 **The Lord will send on you curses, confusion and rebuke in everything you put your hand to, until you are destroyed and come to sudden ruin because of the evil you have done in forsaking him**.

21 The Lord will plague you with diseases until He has destroyed you from the land you are entering to possess.

22 The Lord will strike you with wasting disease, with fever and inflammation, with scorching heat and drought, with blight and mildew, which will plague you until you perish.

23 The sky over your head will be bronze, the ground beneath you iron.

24 The Lord will turn the rain of your country into dust and powder; it will come down from the skies until you are destroyed.

25 The Lord will cause you to be defeated before your enemies. You will come at them from one direction but flee from them in seven, and you will become a thing of horror to all the kingdoms on earth.

26 Your carcasses will be food for all the birds of the air and the beasts of the earth, and there will be no one to frighten them away.

27 The Lord will afflict you with the boils of Egypt and with tumors, festering sores and the itch, from which you cannot be cured.

28 The Lord will afflict you with madness, blindness and confusion of mind.

29 At midday you will grope about like a blind man in the dark. You will be unsuccessful in everything you do; day after day you will be oppressed and robbed, with no one to rescue you.

30 You will be pledged to be married to a woman, but another will take her and ravish her. You will build a house, but you will not even begin to enjoy its fruit. Your ox will be slaughtered before your eyes, but you will eat none of it.

31 Your donkey will be forcibly taken from you and will not be returned. Your sheep will be given to your enemies, and no one will rescue them.

32 Your sons and daughters will be given to another nation, and you will wear out your eyes watching for them day after day, powerless to lift a hand.

33 A people that you do not know will eat what your land and labor produce, and you will have nothing but cruel oppression all your days.

34 The sights you see will drive you mad.

35 The Lord will afflict your knees and legs with painful boils that cannot be cured, spreading from the soles of your feet to the top of your head.

36 The Lord will drive you and the king you set over you to a nation unknown to you or your fathers. There you will worship other gods, gods of wood and stone.

37 You will become a thing of horror and an object of scorn and ridicule to all the nations where the Lord will drive you.

38 You will sow much seed in the field but you will harvest little, because locusts will devour it.

39 You will plant vineyards and cultivate them but you will not drink the wine or gather the grapes, because worms will eat them.

40 You will have olive trees throughout your country but you will not use the oil, because the olives will drop off.

41 You will have sons and daughters but you will not keep them because they will go into captivity.

42 Swarms of locusts will take over all your trees and the crops of your land.

43 The alien who lives among you will rise above you higher and higher, but you will sink lower and lower.

44 He will lend to you, but you will not lend to him. He will be the head but you will be the tail.

45 All these curses will come upon you. They will pursue you and overtake you until you are destroyed, because you did not obey the Lord your God and observe the commands and decrees He gave you.

46 They will be a sign and a wonder to you and your descendants forever.

47 Because you did not serve the Lord your God joyfully and gladly in the time of prosperity,

48 therefore in hunger and thirst, in nakedness and dire poverty, you will serve the enemies the Lord sends against you. He will put an iron yoke on your neck until He has destroyed you.

49 The Lord will bring a nation against you from far away, from the ends of the earth, like an eagle swooping down, a nation whose language you will not understand,

50 a fierce-looking nation without respect for the old or pity for the young.

51 They will devour the young of your livestock and the crops of your land until you are destroyed. They will leave you no grain, new wine or oil, nor any calves of your herds or lambs of your flocks until you are ruined. They will lay siege to all the cities throughout your land until the high fortified walls in which you trust fall down.

52 They will besiege all the cities throughout the land the Lord your God is giving you.

53 Because of the suffering that your enemy will inflict on you during the siege, you will eat the fruit of the womb, the flesh of the sons and daughters the Lord your God has given you.

54 Even the most gentle and sensitive man among you will have no compassion on his own brother or the wife he loves or his surviving children,

55 and he will not give to one of them any of the flesh of his children that he is eating. It will be all he has left because of the suffering your enemy will inflict on you during the siege of all your cities.

56 The most gentle and sensitive woman among you – so sensitive and gentle that she would not venture to touch the ground with the sole of her foot – will begrudge the husband she loves and her son or daughter

57 the afterbirth from her womb and the children she bears. For she intends to eat them secretly during the siege and in the distress that your enemy will inflict on you in your cities.

58 If you do not carefully follow all the words of this law, which are written in this book, and do not revere this glorious and awesome name – the Lord your God –

59 the Lord will send fearful plagues on you and your descendents, harsh and prolonged disasters, and severe and lingering illnesses.

60 He will bring upon you all the diseases of Egypt that you dreaded, and they will cling to you.

61 The Lord will also bring on you every kind of sickness and disaster not recorded in this Book of the Law, until you are destroyed.

62 You who were as numerous as the stars in the sky will be left but few in number, because you did not obey the Lord your God.

63 Just as it pleased the Lord to make you prosper and increase in number, so it will please Him to ruin and destroy you. You will be uprooted from the land you are entering to possess.

64 Then the Lord will scatter you among all nations, from one end of the earth to the other. There you will worship other gods – gods of wood and stone, which neither you nor your fathers have known.

65 Among those nations you will find no repose, no resting place for the sole of your foot. There the Lord will give you an anxious mind, eyes weary with longing, and a despairing heart.

66 You will live in constant suspense, filled with dread both night and day, never sure of your life.

67 In the morning you will say, "If only it were evening!" and in the evening, "If only it were morning!" – because of the terror that will fill your hearts and the sights that your eyes will see.

68 The Lord will send you back in ships to Egypt on a journey I said you should never make again. There you will offer yourselves for sale to your enemies as male and female slaves, but no one will buy you.

All bad or sad things happening or fear of bad or sad things happening are the result of the curse. Poverty, sickness, family problems and all types of fears are the result of the curse. If someone has problem after problem, heartache after heartache, pain after pain—he must realize the curse is operating in his life. He must also examine his life to see how the curse is authorized to operate in his life. Proverbs 26:2 says, "A curse will not come without a cause." Behind every curse there is a reason. The reason lies with the person or someone in his family who is living disobediently to God's ways.

The Generational Curse of Disunity

Again, a generational curse is the devil's destructive plan to devalue a family (parents and children) by means of negative experiences in their lives until that family is destroyed. The generational curse does not just affect you. It also affects your children, your grandchildren and your great-grandchildren.

Disunity is part of the curse. God says it pleases Him when the brethren live together in unity (Ps. 133:1). God says He hates divorce (Mal. 2:16). Yet Grandpa divorced Grandma, Daddy divorced Mama, and Brother divorced his wife. When a person lives disobediently to God's Word in an area and someone in the next generation of that family disobeys God's Word in the same area, the next generation has been cursed. It is a generational curse.

The next generation is not cursed just because the parental generation was cursed. God said He would not destroy children for the sins of parents and He would not destroy parents for the sins of the children (II Chron. 25:4). Children are cursed when they disobey God's Word. The children's generation is cursed when they disobey God's Word just as their parents' generation was cursed when their parents disobeyed God.

The same lie Satan used against Eve is the same lie he uses against families today. The lie he told Eve was that God can't be trusted. As a result of believing that lie, disunity was released on the earth. When Adam and Eve realized there was a consequence to their disobedience they hid. The consequence was evident right away. The Bible says "…their eyes were opened" and what they saw frightened them (Gen. 3:10).

The Lie, the Act, the Fear

Disunity or disobedience causes people to be afraid. Parents have tried to contend with disobedience alone. But there are three forces that must be contended with. Parents must contend with the lie of the disobedience, the act of disobedience, and the fear of rejection. The trouble is not just the act of disobedience. It is the lie, the act and the fear.

Many parents feel like saying "No" is all there is to correcting a child. Sometimes, especially when the child is very young, "no" is all they can understand. But as children get older, parents must be mindful that disobedience does not travel alone. It comes with a lie that the child believes about her parents and it comes with the fear that her parents will reject her.

Many times parents, in trying to correct their child's behavior, make the child feel rejected because they don't deal with the lie about them and the fear of rejection that comes with disobedience. They deal too harshly or too leniently with the disobedience, and the lie and the fear remain. The lie and the fear get stronger and stronger the longer they are not dealt with. The more deceived and the more afraid a child is, the more disobedient he will be.

When my son was three, the nursery age children of our church were to sing Christmas songs in a choir style for the congregation. My son was so afraid to go before the people that he would not "obey" me. He wanted me to carry him. Normally, I would have but I was carrying his baby sister and could not carry them both. His lie was that I was not helping him; therefore, he was not important. This lie had displayed itself through disobedience a few times since my daughter's birth so I recognized it in this setting. After getting him to sit on the risers, I placed my arm around him held him close to me. He was fine. The fear was gone and he even sang some of the songs we had practiced.

Many children are being disobedient because they believe a lie regarding their parents. The greatest needs that children have are for their parents to love, nourish and nurture them. When their needs are not being met consistently, they believe the lie that their parents can't be trusted. Then they disobey. After they disobey, fear of rejection begins to torment them.

Mistakes Happen

When parents are extremely authoritarian or extremely permissive they create a separation or disunity between them and their children. These parents don't give love, nourishment and nurture consistently, which are needed to allow the generational blessing of unity to flow. Authoritarian parents disallow their children the freedom to make mistakes. When children are not free in their hearts to make mistakes, they are afraid to make mistakes and so the fear is compounded. Permissive parents disallow their children the freedom to learn from their mistakes. When children are not wise enough to avoid certain mistakes, they keep making them. When parents are lack in their use of discipline, the lie is compounded.

Deception and fear of rejection are at the root of dysfunctional families and the generational curse. When someone is afraid to make mistakes or does not learn from his mistakes, he does not behave in the freedom which God intended him to behave. It was for freedom that Christ made us free (Gal. 5:1). Christ made us free to make mistakes and free to learn from those mistakes. We are not to be afraid of making mistakes, nor are we to be flippant toward our mistakes.

Many times mistakes are the result of missing the mark. God doesn't hold a hammer over our heads when we make mistakes. He doesn't pat us on the head and send us on our way either. He tells us to repent. When we repent He is faithful and just to forgive us and cleanse us from all unrighteousness (I Jn. 1:9). When we as parents forgive and release our children (or wipe the slate clean) from offending us, fear cannot remain in them. Love covers a multitude of sins (Prov. 10:11).

We Need To Be Good Parents

God's plan for families is only good. When He created families He created them good. His perfect love prevented fear from entering. But when disobedience comes, fear comes with it. If you are a person who knows your parents' forgiveness and release, you will be a parent whose children know your forgiveness and release. Parents are the models for parents. We will parent our children the way our parents parented us. The easiest way to be a good parent is having good parents for models.

Some people feel that because they did not have good parents they can be excused from honoring their parents. They didn't imagine rejection, they lived with rejection. Maybe their parents were extremely authoritarian or extremely permissive. Still this does not excuse a child from honoring his parents. Nor does it excuse a child from growing up to be a good parent.

Although the focus of this book is on your breaking the curse off of your life, parents are held responsible if they modeled the curse to their children. Our parents are responsible for the way they treated, or mistreated, us. Still, if your parents have not broken the curse, you must break it. If your parents have not released you from offenses you committed, all you can do is repent to your parents, if possible, and repent to God. Then accept God's forgiveness and His release.

Cursed people curse people. Hurting people hurt people. Fearful people intimidate other people. You have to want to break all disunity and fear off your life no matter what your parents have done. We cannot live blessed lives if we dishonor our parents. Our children cannot live blessed lives if they dishonor us. Generational curses are the result of children not honoring their parents.

Children Are Not Cursed Until They Disobey God

There is a mystery of iniquity (II Thess. 2:7). We don't know why our kids respond in the same negative way we once did. It is a mystery, but that is what happens. It really is a sad cycle. But it can be turned around with any generation. After Adam and Eve disobeyed God, Cain did not have to also disobey God. When God told him that his offering was not acceptable, he could have brought back an offering that was acceptable (Gen. 4:6-7).

He could have turned things around, but instead he did what his parents had done. He broke unity. His goal was not to break unity with his parents, but when he rejected, acted selfishly toward, and got so angry with Abel that he killed him, Cain broke family unity (Gen. 4:8). The curse of disunity on Adam and Eve became the curse of disunity on Cain. Adam and Eve were driven away from God. Cain was driven away from Adam and Eve (Gen. 4:14). It was a generational curse.

When Cain sinned, the curse of disunity was already in place. It wasn't something God thought up when Cain sinned. The model from God is disobedient people cannot stand in His presence. As parents our disobedient children will not be able to stay in our presence. So when Cain disobeyed God, he was driven away from his family. The curse is self-defeating. If we look at Cain, by his actions he defeated himself. When he denied his involvement in his brother's death, Cain continued to believe a lie. Thus after the punishment was detailed, he responded in fear, "My punishment is greater than I can bear" (Gen. 4:13).

Many people believe that the curse is something that happens to them, but actually the curse is something in you that comes out of you. Jesus said there is nothing outside a man that can defile a man. It is what comes out of man that shows his heart is defiled (Mark 7:14-23).

"I wouldn't hurt myself," you may say. "I am a victim." Not totally true. It may be true that bad things happened to you, but you are responsible for your attitude. The curse of disunity operates or functions through our negative attitudes. You are already cursed if you have a bad attitude. Specifically, when you have confusing behavior, selfish ambition and unrighteous anger, you open the door of your heart for bad things to happen to your life. You close the door of your heart to disunity by loving, nurturing and nourishing your family. At the same time we close the door to generational curses we open the door to generational blessings.

The Generational Curse is Real

My immediate family heritage is of the curse of disunity. People in my family have had a hard time staying connected in intimate relationships. My parents are divorced. My oldest brother is divorced. My younger brother has been divorced twice. This is a curse. It certainly isn't being blessed when marriages end in divorce.

I have been married over a decade, the longest of any member of my immediate family. Still, in the early years of our marriage my husband and I both felt strained from the curse of disunity pulling our hearts. When the curse is on your family, you must resist it. Some people think there is no such thing as a curse. They think some of the bad things that have happened have been by coincidence.

Nothing happens by coincidence. Just as there is a specific plan of blessing, there is also a specific plan of curses. People choose the blessings or they choose the curses (Deut. 30:19). The blessing doesn't come by accident. It comes as planned. The curse doesn't come by accident. It comes as planned. If we choose to honor our parents, we will be blessed as planned. If we choose to dishonor our parents we will be cursed as planned.

I attribute my ability to stay married to obeying God, having a godly husband, and having a godly mother. Mother taught me unity. She and I lived together until my mid-twenties when I married. Although my brothers and I have the same mother, we do not have this same testimony. I don't write this to condemn her or any parent whose children have had or are having a hard time in long-term relationships, yet my brothers can attribute having gone through multiple marriages to not obeying God, having ungodly wives and having an ungodly mother. We could say it also was due to not having a godly father. Still, Mother was a single parent so the responsibility of child-rearing was on her. (Single parents, as hard as it is to raise children alone, you are still held responsible to teach your children the blessing of unity.)

Mother came to Christ when I was around eleven years old and I followed suit soon after that. My brothers did not follow suit. When Mother came to Christ she much more wanted unity with her children; however, my brothers, being late teenagers when she was saved, had already experienced a great deal of disunity. They loved Mother, but they had learned how to detach themselves.

People learn to detach, or disunite, as children. You are not an adult when you learn to detach. If you detach from your parents, you will detach easily from every other relationship that you have. When you detach from your parents, not only will your employment suffer, your marriage will suffer and your children will suffer.

God's Word says to honor your father and mother and it will be well with you. My brothers' marriages did not end well because they dishonored God. They dishonored God when they dishonored Mother way back in their pre-married life (Gen. 17:2). Ultimately, every relationship we have will be filtered through our relationship with God. There is nothing our parents can do to us that should stop us from trusting God. There is nothing we can do as parents and as children that should stop our children and our parents from trusting God.

God Can Heal Your Family

Knowing this is not a license to mistreat your children or an excuse for the times your parents mistreated you. The point is "there is therefore now no condemnation to those who love the Lord and are called according to His purpose" (Rom. 8:1). We as parents and as children need to repent for the things we have done wrong to our children and to our parents (Ezek. 14:6). After that we need to get our attitudes in line with the Word of God. Satan knows if he can convince people to stay in a state of sorrow or condemnation for the wrong things they have done or have had done to them, they still will not be able to overcome the curse of disunity. He knows as long as the lie and the fear prevail disunity will continue to be a problem in a family.

Disunity puts rips in people's hearts. God loves your family so much. His plan is to use the healing power of unity to sew up any rips. His plan is to use the healing power of unity to make you and your household whole (Acts 16:31). God is the One who heals the brokenhearted (Ps. 147:3). We must allow God to heal our broken hearts so we can be people who forgive and release the breakers of our hearts. We must allow God to heal our broken hearts so we can become whole people.

The praise report is that now one of my brothers is a Christian and he has a growing relationship with the Lord, his father and mother, his godly wife and child. At one time disunity was being practiced, but now unity is being practiced. There is still time to turn things around in your family. If your children are very young, they may never even realize that the curse of disunity had ever touched your family because you have flowed in the blessings of unity for so long. If your children are older, you need to explain to them how the curse of disunity has touched your family and how it has touched them. Then show them how easy it is to turn things around.

Teach Your Child to Honor You and God

Because parent-child relationships are the first or primary relationships that children will have for many years, parents are to teach their children how to stay rightly related to them. The only way children can stay rightly related to their parents is for them to honor their parents. If your child does not honor you, that child will have no real foundation of being rightly related with other people. If she does not honor you, she will not honor God.

God gets honor when our children honor us. God says when our children honor Him, He will honor them (I Sam. 2:30). He will honor them to be unified with their families. He will honor them to be unified with Himself. When parents and children honor God they will demonstrate the same kind of unity with their families as Jesus demonstrated He had with His Father (Jn. 17:6-9).

Confusing behaviors (criticism, unresolved issues, misunderstandings and impatience), selfish ambition and unrighteous anger are the behaviors found in disunity; however, the breakdown in unity usually begins with ungodly correction. Here are a few godly ways to administer correction:

1. Acknowledge that there are no perfect parents. Sometimes we put our parents on a pedestal and they can't make any mistakes. They can and they will. If you are a parent, you can and you will.
2. Acknowledge that there are no perfect children. Allow them the freedom to make mistakes. Talk to them to help them to be wise against making avoidable mistakes.
3. Resist being extremely authoritarian or permissive. All of us, according to our personality, will have a style of parenting that slants one way or the other. Make it your goal to be balanced in your parenting style.
4. Ask your children to tell you what they have done wrong when you think they have disobeyed. Don't simply accuse your children. Remember, they are innocent until proven guilty. Also, remember that Satan is the accuser of the

brethren. Remember: when you are accusatory, you are being more like the devil than God.

5. Have them tell you why what they did was wrong. Have family rules that everyone knows. Don't try to come up with rules right on the spot. Give your child every opportunity to be obedient. He can't obey rules he doesn't know.

6. Have your child repent. Many people have a hard time saying "I am sorry." Even more people have a hard time saying "I was wrong, please forgive me." But in order for them to revoke the lie, they must admit they were wrong. In order to avoid fear they must ask for forgiveness.

7. Forgive your children when they disobey. Tell them that you forgive them. Children are children and they have so much to learn. When they make mistakes it is not the end of the world. Forgive and release them easily.

8. Determine what the disciplinary action will be. Remember the point of correction is to make your child wise according to the Word of God.

9. Often remind your children before and after any negative interactions with them that you love them. Often remind yourself before and after any negative interactions with your children that you are administering disciplinary actions to keep them from believing a lie and from being afraid of rejection.

Regarding spanking, I believe there are times and reasons for spanking. Proverbs 22:15 says, "Foolishness is bound up in the heart of a child; The rod of correction will drive it far from him." However, because spanking is the most unwanted interaction you can have with your child, spanking should be used as a last resort. If you spend a lot of time loving, nurturing and nourishing your children, you will have fewer (I didn't say non-existent) negative interactions with your children.

God's Word on Believing in Discipline:

My children shall be taught of the Lord and great shall be their peace. (Is. 54:13 NKJV)

Correct your son and he will give you rest; yes, he will give delight to your soul. (Prov. 29:17 NKJV)

God has not given me the spirit of fear, but of power and of love and of a sound mind. (II Tim. 1:7 NKJV)

Even though I walk through the valley of the shadow of death I will fear no evil, for you art with me; Your rod and Your staff, they comfort me. (Ps. 23:4)

God will never leave me nor forsake me. (Deut. 31:6)

Ridding Confusing Behaviors

Generally, confusion means not knowing what to do. In terms of relationships it means not knowing the right way to behave. This chapter is about the confusing behaviors that cause children to question their parents' love for them.

Many parents do not relate to their children correctly. As a result the children do not relate to their parents correctly. Those children grow up not knowing how to relate to their spouses and children correctly. The generational curse can come into the family line by way of confusion.

When people honor God's Word and their parents, their other relationships will be more valuable. When parents focus on loving their children instead of confusing them, their children will grow up focusing on loving their spouse and children and not confusing them.

God is not the author of confusion, but of peace (I Cor. 14:33). Many families are not living in peace because God is not ruling the household. Confusion is. Parents are confused about their children's behavior. Children are confused about their parent's behavior. Neither understands why the other is doing the negative things that bring about negative outcomes in the family. When the curse of disunity is confronted, confusion will be uprooted and family members will enjoy peaceful relationships with each other. When the curse of disunity is confronted, both parents and children will have more understanding regarding their own responses.

As I have already mentioned, children use behavior to test the love level in the family. The illustration below depicts what happens when parents wrongly react to their children's misbehavior, or negative behavior.

ILLUSTRATION 4

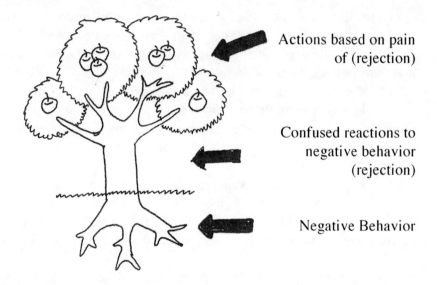

Actions based on pain
of (rejection)

Confused reactions to
negative behavior
(rejection)

Negative Behavior

The roots of negative behavior may be covert or overt, just as a tree's roots can be seen above ground or hidden underground. Children may be withdrawn or they may be boisterous. They may be low achievers or high achievers. Every time parents mishandle their children's negative behavior they set in rejection to be the underlying trunk to their children's lives. The fruit (the apples) of the children's lives reveal if the children are acting out from the pain of rejection.

People under the curse of disunity are responding to the painful experiences in their lives. What is your threshold for pain? Some people have a very low tolerance for pain. Other people have a very high tolerance for pain. Irregardless of your tolerance for pain, when someone confuses you by mistreating you, or rejecting you, you feel emotional pain. When you are rejected you will feel hurt.

All throughout one's life, from conception to the grave, everyone will have to fight the pain of rejection. There is no escaping it. Rejection is part of the fallen nature of the world and imperfect people (Gen. 3:16). Rejection means to refuse to take, agree to, or to rebuff. It also means to deny acceptance, care, or love to someone.

Even if your parents were very loving, they rejected (refused to take, agree to, rebuffed) the things you did that they did not like. They may have even rejected (denied acceptance, care, love to) you. Even though you love your children, you rejected (refused to take, agree to, rebuffed) the things they did that you did not like. You may even have rejected (denied acceptance, care, love to) your children.

Rejection Starts at an Early Age

Satan's plan is for families not to get along (Matt. 12:25). Accordingly, he uses rejection to confuse people about their parents' love for them. Parents have to be very careful during times they dislike their child's behavior not to reject (deny acceptance, care, love to) their child. When parents discipline out of anger, the children are confused and believe that their parents do not like them, not just their behavior.

Some people use anger to try to produce peace in their homes. They stomp their feet. They slam doors. They yell. They may spank in anger. They may even use the silent treatment. But instead of producing peaceful children, they are producing fearful children. Instead of producing peaceful children, they are producing confused children.

We live in a very selfish society that says, "I want what I want. I want it now and if I don't get it, I will reject you. I won't like you." When my son was in kindergarten I began to notice him saying, "I don't like so and so." Really, he was saying 'I don't like what so and so did.' But in his immaturity he simply threw out the baby with the bathwater. He simply rejected kids who did things he did not like.

Most people believe rejection of others starts at an age when we are old enough to understand the ramifications of it. However, I noticed my five-year-old son rejecting people. Babies can reject people. Parents can reject their children in the womb. Some parents reject their children because they wanted a boy and they got a girl. Some parents reject their children because they didn't want any more children or they did not want to have another child when they did.

Being born close to a sibling can cause rejection to work against one or both of the children. I knew a mother of a one-year-old daughter who gave birth to a son. The son had colic. Having the two so close together, having their needs so close together, two in diapers, caused this mom some stress. However, when the son developed colic the stress was magnified. The mom was not able to rest well. She was physically and emotionally tired. Colic is a miserable condition for both mom and baby. Some moms reject their babies when they cry a lot. I am not saying this mom rejected her baby. I know she had a lot of physical and emotional support. Still, with colic, the crying is excessive and mothers can begin to get "tired" of trying to stop all that crying and subtly or even overtly reject that child.

It is understandable that a parent will get tired of trying to correct their child's behavior, but if a child cries a lot, there is something wrong with that child. Many children today are "crying out" with bad behavior. Something is wrong with that child; however, parents are tired of trying to correct their children's behavior.

Many children are not cooperating with their parents and their parents have grown weary in trying to correct their behavior. They have stopped trying to correct their children. Mom, I speak strength into you. Dad, I speak strength into you. Grandparent, I speak strength into you. Galatians 6:9 says, "Be not weary in your well doing for you will reap if you faint not." As parents our main concern should not be how tired we are. Our main concern should be to find out what is wrong with our children. Why is that baby, that child, or that teenager crying so much?

When a child is rejected by her parents, a spirit of rejection can enter her soul. Again, it may have entered in the womb. Unwed mothers particularly usually do not impart acceptance into their children right away because they do not want to have children at that time.

If you believe that people do not like you, people will not forgive you, people are hard to get along with or people are impatient with you, you are dealing with a spirit of rejection. The spirit of rejection causes people not to like you. It also causes you not to like people. Criticism, unresolved conflicts, misunderstandings and impatience are the avenues in which the spirit of rejection is imparted to people. Rejection causes people to react to life negatively.

Criticism Causes Confusion

When parents criticize their children, they are not producing peace in their children. Criticism is the act of making judgments, the act of finding fault or disapproval. In telling someone something negative about his or her behavior we must beware of judging him or her. God says we are not to judge others (Matt. 7:1). He is the only judge (Is. 33:22).

Children know when they are under the law and Judge Mom or Judge Dad is handing down their sentence. If parents are constantly trying to fix their children, they are unconsciously or consciously rejecting their child's personality. How many times a day, a week, a month do you tell your children "no"? If it seems like it is many times a day, or many times a week or many times a month, then it is time for you to try a new strategy with your children. It is time to say "Yes."

How many parents really want their children to be happy? Children are very creative little people. How about saying "yes" to your child's desires for the next 24 hours (only say no if the activity is harmful to the child, the child's sibling, you or anything valuable or precious)? Fear is trying to rise up in some of you reading this. What? Say yes to my children? What? Let my children lead me? Yes, say yes to your children. Yes, let your children lead you (Isa. 11:6). This will be hard to do if you were disunited from your parents. This will be hard if your parents said no to you a lot.

God has not given you the spirit of fear, but of love, of power and of a sound mind (II Tim. 1:9). I am not advocating doormatism. I am advocating peace. When there are issues that disturb your peace, you need to discuss them. If there is always an issue under the table, there will not be peace at the table. Resolve the problems. If there is a problem with the children, parents need to talk it over with their children. Resolve the problems.

Many people often confuse criticism with resolution. When we criticize our family members we may be telling them what we don't like about them, but we are not producing peace in them. We are producing fear. As mentioned in the last chapter, ungodly discipline produces fear. In the same way criticism is used to attempt to change a person's behavior. When we seek resolutions with our family members we will produce peace.

Resolutions seek to bring problems to an end. Criticism simply says there is a problem. Proverbs 29:17 says, "Correct your children and they will give thee rest; yes, they will give delight unto your soul." Doesn't that sound wonderful? God's plan for you and your children is that they would give delight unto your soul. When the parents' plan of handling problems is to criticize instead of seeking resolutions, they will produce confused children.

Confused children constantly test the boundaries the parents have set up. They do not give delight unto their parents' souls. They do not give their parents rest. These children were not corrected. These children did not receive resolutions to problems. They were criticized and intimidated and now are unable to discern the right way to behave in relationships.

Criticism hurts the most because it usually attacks our weaknesses. We are all weak in some area. So when one of our family members magnifies our weakness we get defensive. When one of our family members comes across as the judge, we almost have no choice but to come back across as the defendant. It becomes a standoff, you against me and me against you.

Judgment is a catalyst in producing disunity. The key to keep unity intact in a family is by possessing an attitude to always want to resolve conflicts and to not stand as the judge of your family members. When conflicts are resolved peace will always be restored to that relationship.

Have you ever heard the saying, "All minds clear"? "All minds clear" means everything that relates to a specific issue that needs to be said has been said. Peace will be restored when one party has listened to the other party's grievance. They are not communicating, "You are wrong for behaving that way," but "Did something happen at school today? Tell me about it."

A mother may say to her son as soon as he gets home from school, "You are so lazy. You didn't take out the trash this morning." That is criticism. The son may go to his room and slam the door. "Get off my back, nag," he murmurs. He criticizes her back, not out loud, but mostly in his heart and the issue is never dealt with. Well, what is the issue? With this example, the mother is frustrated that the trash was not taken out to the curb and now the garage is smelly. Instead of criticizing or accusing her son of laziness, she should pray for her son and allow the Holy Spirit to direct her on how and when to discuss the issue with her son.

When she discusses her concerns about the trash with her son, her tone will not be accusatory and her timing will be right. She should start by telling him the facts of her frustrations. She could say, "Mike, the garage smelled very stinky when I got home from work today."

That is the fact. There is no accusation in her speech, so by bringing up the subject she is not rejecting him. When she didn't reject him, he didn't feel defensive. He could then just apologize for forgetting to take the trash out. When his mother didn't accuse him he didn't feel like he had to defend himself. When she didn't reject him because he forgot to take the trash out he felt no pain.

After the problem was defined, the conflict could be resolved. After the problem was defined, potential solutions could be discussed. What can we do to prevent this from happening again? God knows the answer to every problem. He wants us to know the answer to our problems.

Prayer should always be a part of the solution. Many times prayer is needed to discern the real problem. Forgetting to take the trash out is a problem, but what is the root of forgetfulness? In this case maybe Mike is staying up too late. Maybe he has too many other responsibilities in the morning. Maybe he just doesn't want to take the trash out. Once the real problem is agreed upon, then solutions to the problem can be discussed and the conflict resolved.

Unresolved Conflicts Cause Confusion

Many people get stuck in unresolved conflicts because they do not understand why mistakes or disobedience happens. Parents cannot understand why their son broke the lamp or why their daughter stayed out past curfew. As a result those parents do not forgive. When they choose not to forgive they are operating in the generational curse.

Unforgiveness prevents relationships from being as good as they were before. Children are confused when parents don't forgive them. The children cannot understand why their relationship with their parents cannot be as good as it was before the lamp was broken or curfew was broken.

Many families split apart because of unresolved conflicts. They stay focused on "why that happened." They stay focused on the result of what happened. They cannot seem to forgive the children for what has happened and release the children from mistakes or acts of disobedience. Some people would rather reject family members than forgive and release them.

Although rejection causes emotional pain, many children actually feel the pain in their physical bodies. The pain of rejection can be felt inside of a child's heart, or stomach, or head. Our emotions are so connected to our bodies that if we listen to our bodies we can know how we are doing emotionally. There are many people who are sick in their bodies because they were rejected or they fear rejection. Heart disease and ulcers have been medically linked to emotional problems.

Among the medical community, it has been well known that health problems can be genetic, i.e., passed down from generation to generation. That is why a doctor will ask his patient to give a medical history. The medical history not only looks at how you have been feeling, but also looks at how your parents have been feeling.

The emotional problems that cause some of the health problems are also "genetic" among family members. Rejection can be passed down from generation to generation. Parents can pass down the rejection they felt as children to their children.

Many people are angry at their parents because their parents rejected them. In trying to produce peace, many parents only produced accusations or rejection of their children. We all have reasons to forgive our parents. Our children will have reasons to forgive us. Parents can only do what they know to do. Unfortunately, however, as Hosea 4:6 says, "My people are destroyed for the lack of knowledge." Some parents don't know their behavior is encouraging their children to disunite from them.

Misunderstandings Cause Confusion

Misunderstandings often lead to confusion. When we need to understand our parents or our children, we should be simple in our search for the truth. Many times we want something or want to know something, but we don't come right out and say it. Many times when we are not specific we cause misunderstandings.

Recently, my son was taking a bath and I had already told him once it was time for him to come out. My daughter was waiting to take her bath. So after a while I started to notice he still wasn't out. I did not understand why he wasn't out yet. I knew he heard me say it was time for him to come out. So I knocked on the bathroom door and my initial plan was to tell him to get out...again. But instead I asked him, "Are you coming out?" This was a yes and no question. This was not something I said to accuse him of dawdling. I didn't say anything to put him down. It was a simple yes and no question. To which he answered yes, but he'd just washed his hair and so forth. After my son's explanation, I no longer felt confused about his behavior.

When misunderstandings occur we can still patiently wait for the truth to come out. Sometimes in our quest to be right, we rush our family members. Remember: the goal in our family relationships is not to be the one who is right all the time. The goal is peace.

Impatience Causes Confusion

Impatience also leads to confusion. Impatience causes your family members to question your motives. Have you ever been driving on the road and suddenly hit a pothole? The car shakes. You shake. You wonder, *What happened?* If the size of the pothole is small, you may barely notice it. However, if the size and shape of the pothole causes your tire to go flat, you get mad and angrily say, "The city is neglectful. They are going to pay for this."

When you are impatient with your family members you are *suddenly* annoyed with their weakness, immature or "slow" behavior. Impatient behavior damages your family members because of its quick turn from pleasant to unpleasant. Your family members are not expecting that unpleasant reaction from you; therefore, they do not understand why you have mistreated them.

Your impatient behavior forces your family members to make a decision. Are they going to forgive you quickly for being impatient with them? Are they going to resent you for being impatient with them? Or are they going to believe something is wrong with them? Are they going to be confused?

So what started as a nice drive, a nice conversation, a nice day suddenly feels like a bomb has gone off when we act impatiently. Our children, our spouse and our parents will respond to our impatience. Our impatience can give our children, our spouse and our parents an excuse to disunite from us.

When a person is impatient with one of his family members and feels he can justify mistreatment, that person is not confused. That person is deceived (Obad. 3). A confused person doesn't realize he is doing something wrong. In a court of law to determine if someone is sane enough to stand trial, a person is tested to see if she can discern the difference between right and wrong. A confused person cannot. To a confused person the truth is mixed up or jumbled. A deceived person knows what he is doing is wrong. The deception is that he tries to justify why he did something wrong. He knows he is wrong, but somehow it is okay.

A daughter wants her father to fix her broken doll. He says he can't right now, but he will later. The daughter knows she should be respectful towards her dad, but she tells him he is mean. She whines. She yells. She throws the doll down. She is wrong. The Bible says children are to honor their father and mother (Ex. 20:12, Deut. 5:16, Matt. 15:4, Eph. 6:2). For her to yell at her dad is not respectful. If she yells at him and doesn't know she is wrong, she is confused. If she yells at him and knows she is wrong, she is deceived. Either way she has not discerned that maintaining peace with her father is the right thing to do.

Beware the Trap of Confusion

If you have ever watched a college basketball game, you have inevitably seen the defensive play called "the trap." This is a designed defensive play called near the end of the half or near the end of a game. Whenever I have seen the trap I have understood it to be a way to confuse the player with the ball so that he loses it.

The trap begins as soon as a player on Team A inbounds the ball to one of his teammates. When the Team A teammate touches the ball, Team B will immediately have two players guard Team A player instead of the usual one player. The Team B players wave their hands up and down and side to side fast so that Team A player cannot pass it to one of his teammates. And because there are two players, the Team A player can't easily dribble down the court. The Team A player has no where to go with the ball. He is trapped.

The right thing to do in that situation is to dribble up the court quickly before that second defender comes, pass the ball quickly to one of his teammates or if that team has time outs available, call a time out. But in the heat of the moment, Team A player can get confused and travel (taking too many steps without dribbling the ball), charge against (run into) one of the players on Team B or in some way turn the ball over. Turning the ball over is the wrong thing for the Team A player to do for his team. Turning the ball over could cause his team to lose the game.

When you feel confusion know that the devil has set out a trap for you (Ps. 119:110). He wants you to lose your peace. He wants you to hurt your family. He wants you to lose your family. When you feel confusion remember that your goal and God's goal for you is that you maintain your peace. Your goal and God's goal is that you keep your family.

Unless you have practiced "the trap" and quickly recognize the enemy attempting to confuse you, you won't immediately be able to do the right thing. You won't be able to maintain your peace. So here is a drill: Say your father was upset at you and angrily says, "Be quiet. You talk too much. I don't want to hear anything else you have to say!" That is rejection coming through criticism. Quickly now, what do you do? Quickly, instead of becoming defensive or behaving disrespectfully, ask the Holy Spirit to tell you how you should respond. Colossians 4:6 says, "Let your conversation be gracious and effective so that you will have the right answer for everyone." (NLT)

In this example, the Holy Spirit may tell you to be quiet. He may say to do what your father said to do. Later, He may lead you to talk to your father about the way he talked to you. The Holy Spirit will lead you to seek resolution.

If you make it a habit to ask the Holy Spirit to tell you how to respond, you will respond with peace. You can avoid confusion. Confusion in your life causes you to mistreat people. Confusion in your life causes you to reject others. When I understood how to respond with peace to my mother, even though she and I have different personalities and life experiences, we enjoyed greater peace in our relationship. I do not have to agree with everything she says to maintain the peace, but I must respond respectfully to her to maintain the peace.

When we are disrespectful to our parents, we are not promoting peace. We are promoting confusion in our own lives. First Timothy 2:2 says, "Lead a quiet and peaceable life." Hebrews 12:14 says, "Follow peace with all men." Jesus said, "Blessed are the peace-makers" (Matt. 5:9). People who do not promote peace do not live a quiet life. They live a confused, upset life.

Many times we want to justify why we are not walking in peace. Peace is a fruit of the Spirit of God (Gal. 5:22). Therefore, if we have the Spirit of God inside of us, we cannot justify not walking in peace. Certainly, there will be people who because of their person-alities and life experiences will squeeze your fruit harder than other people, but God's Word is forever settled in heaven (Ps. 119:89). You have peace inside of you. When someone needs an example of peace, they will squeeze your fruit. Give them peace-juice when they squeeze your peace.

The Holy Spirit Is the Umpire

The Holy Spirit will enlighten you when you are mistreating (not giving peace to) your family members (Jn. 14:26). However, you can ignore Him. Your conscience can be so seared that even though God is speaking, you can't hear Him. Seared means to make callous or unfeeling; harden. A seared conscience comes from ignoring God when He has tried to correct you. You know you shouldn't have said that, but...

If you know you shouldn't have said that, the Holy Spirit is telling you to repent. If you don't repent, the next time you say something that you shouldn't have said, the Holy Spirit will not speak as loudly to tell you that what you said was wrong. It isn't that He isn't speaking. It is that you are not able to hear Him speaking clearly. God told Isaiah to tell the people in 6:9-10:

Be ever hearing, but never understanding
Be ever seeing, but never perceiving.
Make the heart of this people calloused;
Make their ears dull
And close their eyes.
Otherwise they might see with their eyes,
Hear with their ears,
Understand with their hearts,
And turn and be healed (*in their relationships*).

Parents, do not allow your children to ignore you. My children know I mean what I say. They know if I say stop, I mean stop. They know if I say sit down, I mean sit down. Jesus said let your yes be yes and no be no (Matt. 5:37). Why? Anything else will foster confusion. If I say stop, but my children do not believe me and don't stop, it is because I have said stop in the past and they didn't obey and I didn't enforce my command. They are confused. They are unable to discern the right thing to do regarding me. They knew what I said, but they didn't know I meant it.

In the same way with God our Father, if the Holy Spirit offers us correction and we ignore His correction, we are confused. We reject God when we don't believe His Word. His Word says those who are willing and obedient will eat the good of the land (Is. 1:19). His Word says we can break the curse of disunity by honoring our father and mother (Eph. 6:2). Do you believe it?

Unbelief is a very difficult mindset to overcome. It comes as a result of not believing our parents. So a word to parents, don't play games with your children. I am not talking about games like catch or Scrabble™. I am talking about mind games. Parents, consistently follow-through in what you tell your children you will do and what you tell your children to do. If you don't, you set your children up for confusion to control their lives.

Godly Wisdom Overcomes Confusion

As Christian parents we can ask the Holy Spirit to show us the reason for the confusing behavior. We can ask the Holy Spirit for wisdom. James 1:5-8 says:

If any of you lacks wisdom, he should ask God, who gives generously to all without finding fault, and it will be given to him.

But when he asks, he must believe and not doubt, because he who doubts is like a wave of the sea, blown and tossed by the wind. (*Sounds tiring, doesn't it?*)

That man should not think he will receive anything from the Lord; he is a double-minded man, unstable in all he does.

James 3:13-18 says:

Who is wise and understanding among you? Let him show it by his good life, by deeds done in the humility that comes from wisdom.

But if you harbor bitter envy and selfish ambition in your hearts, do not boast about it or deny the truth.

Such "wisdom" does not come down from heaven but is earthly, unspiritual, of the devil.

For where you have envy and selfish ambition, there you find disorder and every evil practice. (*There you find the curse of disunity.*)

But the wisdom that comes from heaven is first of all pure; then peace-loving, considerate, submissive, full of mercy and good fruit, impartial and sincere.

Peacemakers who sow in peace raise a harvest of righteousness.

God does not want parents to be confused. There is wisdom available to us when we seek it. The good news is the mom with the colicky son sought advice, went to the health food store and bought a natural product which helped the baby digest his food better. The excessive crying stopped. When the excessive crying stopped the mom was able to rest better. Peace was restored to that relationship.

We can get so focused on trying to fix what is wrong that we overlook our child's feelings. Sometimes we may even say to our child, "What is wrong with you?" A child cannot usually tell us what is wrong. Even teenagers may not know exactly what is wrong. But through their symptoms, which are usually peaks of negative behavior, they will show us something is wrong. The boundary is being tested. If we can easily fix the child's symptoms or negative behavior, that is, get our child to stop excessively crying, talking back, ignoring our instructions, fine. No problem. But if we can't easily fix the negative behavior, rejection for the child can set in.

We want to be happy. Sometimes our concern for our happiness causes us to overlook the happiness of others. Sometimes our concern for our happiness causes us to overlook the happiness of our children. But as I mentioned earlier in this book, we should try to help others be happy. We are blessed to be a blessing (Gen. 22:17).

Parents want to be a blessing to their children. They want peace with their children, but many parents are confused. Their confusion is evident when they reject their child and think that rejection will produce peace. Rejection will not produce peace. Rejection may make a child too afraid to talk to his parents, but it will not produce peace in that child. It may make a child be quiet, but it will not produce peace.

For my son's fifth birthday, my mother bought him a LarryMobile™. After she gave it to him, Andrew was very quiet. You could tell his entire soul was at peace. He had gotten what he wanted for his birthday. Andrew wanted a LarryMobile™ for a long time. By nourishing Andrew's soul, Mother led her grandson into peace.

There is a quietness of the soul that is produced by peace. However, real peace cannot be falsely manufactured. Many people try to get peace through alcohol or some illicit relationship. However, true peace can only be produced when one receives love, nourishment and nurture from God, your family members and significant others in your life.

Love Overcomes Rejection

God loves you (Is. 43:4). That has been said so much that it is almost like a cliché. But it is such a profound statement that it could be said a thousand times before we would even begin to understand it. God loves you. If you have experienced a lot of rejection, you may need to say 'God loves me' a thousand times to help you believe in God's love.

God loves you and has a good plan for you no matter what your past has been (Jer. 29:11). When you gave your heart to the Lord you exchanged your old way of life for his new way of life. You exchanged your old way of thinking for His new way of thinking. When you received His new life He poured His love for you into your heart. When you receive His new way of thinking you will pour love into your family members. Receive it. Believe it.

Rejection is as universal a term as love. However, it is only a symptom of a deeper problem. Just as love is the root of many healthy emotions, fear is the root of many unhealthy emotions. Fear is at the root of giving and receiving rejection. The fear of rejection is an enemy to receiving God's love. Proverbs 29:25 says the fear of man is a snare to your soul. In other words, when you are afraid someone will hurt you, your soul cannot receive the love of God. You can only receive God's love by faith. Just as you got saved by faith, all of the other promises of God can only be received by faith.

God is love and He loves us more than any person on earth could ever love us (I Jn. 4:8, 16). There is no love that compares to God's love for us (Jer. 31:3). Inside each one of us, we have a place that only God can satisfy. Your spouse can't do it. Your children can't do it. Your parents can't do it. It is an "only God" spot. Some people try to do everything they can to reject their need for God. Some people work a lot. Some people seek pleasure a lot. But until you allow God to fill His place in you, you will never be truly satisfied and you will not stop rejecting others until you are truly satisfied.

Only a person who is full inside of herself can truly be satisfied. Notice I didn't say "full of herself." I can't satisfy me and you can't satisfy me. Only God in me can satisfy and fill me. If I try to satisfy myself, I will only reject myself when I don't feel satisfied. If I allow you to satisfy me, I will only reject you when you don't satisfy me. When I allow God to satisfy me, I will be satisfied. His love is the love that I have been looking for all my life. And out of His love, out of His satisfaction, I can love others.

Christians are to give away God's love (Gal. 5:13). We are to share the love of God with others. We are to share God's love with people who love Him and people who don't love Him. We are to be witnesses of God's love. We are witnesses of God when we love one another. (Jn. 13:35)

Have you ever been thirsty, I mean, really thirsty? Sometimes when I am thirsty I will get some lemonade to drink. Other times when I am thirsty I will get a soda pop. But when I am really thirsty the only thing that can satisfy me is water.

Now I know when I am really thirsty not to even bother with other things to drink. I just need a glass of cold water. Jesus said come to Him all who are thirsty and He will give you water that flows from within yourself, a continual spring (Jn. 7:37-38 NLT). The only way to fill the thirst for love is to allow God to fill us with His love.

Here are some biblical ways to restore a loving heart:

1. Seek God. Always talk to God about the pain of rejection that you feel. Release it to Him. He can handle it. Jesus bore all of your pain, physical, emotional and spiritual, on the cross at Calvary (Is. 53:4-5).
2. Sing to God songs of His love (Ps. 30:4-5).

3. Repent of being critical, unforgiving, misunderstanding, impatient and anything you may have done to cause the person to reject you (remember: no one is perfect) (Acts 17:30).

4. Forgive. Even before you talk to the person and especially if you will not have an opportunity to talk to them, forgive them. Even if they don't say they are sorry, forgive them (Luke 23:34).

5. Tell the person how you feel and ask if they meant to make you feel that way. Don't assume that people are trying to hurt you (Matt. 18:15).

6. Seek resolutions. Understand what the real problem is. Sometimes the problem is hidden under the surface of defensive emotions. When you get to the root of the problem you can receive the answer to the problem. There is an answer to every problem, and for every conflict there can be a peaceful end (I Cor. 9:19).

Confusion and rejection are meant to steal your peace. You need peace to understand how you should respond to others and overcome disunity.

God's Word on Living Wisely with Others:

Call to Me and I will answer and tell you great and unsearchable things you do not know (Jer. 33:3).

By wisdom a house is built, and through understanding it is established; through knowledge its rooms are filled with rare and beautiful treasures (Prov. 24:3).

The wise woman builds her house, but with her own hands the foolish one tears hers down (Prov. 14:1).

Peace I leave with you, My peace I give to you: not as the world giveth, give I unto you. Let not your heart be troubled, neither let it be afraid (Jn. 14:27 KJV).

Ridding Selfish Ambitions

Why are some kids titled "good kids" while others are titled "bad kids"? Are there some "good" people and some "bad" people? No. People are just people. The actions of people display good motives or bad motives. A good kid displays good motives by being obedient. A bad kid displays bad motives by being disobedient. A good kid displays good motives by being respectful. A bad kid displays bad motives by being disrespectful.

What happens when the good kid becomes the bad kid? What happens when a generally respectful kid displays bad motives by being disrespectful? Nothing that is supernatural. This is human nature. The heart of bad motives is selfishness. All of us at times have been selfish. Me first. Consumerism. Self-centeredness. These adjectives all describe what is at the heart of sin. Romans 3:23 says we all have sinned. We all have been selfish.

On more than one occasion we have all been the person with bad motives. The Bible says do nothing out of selfish ambition (Phil. 2:3). We should not think of ourselves more highly than we ought to (Rom. 12:3). In order to break free from the generational curse of broken relationships, it will take some laying down of our lives. It will take some giving up of some of our rights.

Many times selfish people are simply protecting their rights, their opinions, or their status. There may be a legitimate need to protect. There may be a legitimate right to protect. But the selfish person will only think about his legitimate need without thinking of how fulfillment of his need will affect the rest of the family.

Children have to be taught to consider others. As children we are born selfish. We cry when we don't get our way. We cry when someone won't give us the toy we want. One of the first concepts parents attempt to teach their toddlers in social training is to share. Parents teach this principle through example and instruction. Children watch parents very closely to see how they share.

God Does Not Have Any Favorites

Children are also watching to see if the parents are playing favorites among the siblings. There should be no favorite child in your house because you love all of your children with the same kind of love. You cannot treat all of your children the same because some are older than others, but you can treat each one fairly. When children feel like they have to grab in order to have anything they will grow up to be very selfish. Children who grab do not trust their parents. Children who grab do not trust God.

God does not play favorites. He is an equal opportunity God. He will give us what we ask for when we don't ask with selfish motives (Jas. 4:3).

A few years ago I saw on James Robison's TV program, *Life Today,* his ministry reaching out to feed poor people in Africa. When this ministry first started reaching out to the people with the food there was such need that the people were pushing each other, trying to be sure to get some. Later, the program showed that the ministry had stuck with that group of people and when it was time to distribute the food, the people waited in an orderly fashion. They waited their turn.

The main reason I believe people are selfish all over the world is because they don't know who they are; therefore, they don't know how to receive what God has for them. They don't know that God has a terrific plan and many blessings for their lives. There can be a generational curse of selfishness in a family. Grandma was self-centered. Daddy is self-centered. Junior is self-centered. Instead of them giving their parents honor, each generation only wanted honor for themselves.

Who Are You?

The curse of selfishness can be found in any home. It can be found in a black family. It can be found in a white family. It can be found in a rich family. It can be found in a poor family. It can be

118

found in a family where everyone is healthy. It can be found in a family where someone is sick. Selfishness is not limited to circumstances, for it is based on not knowing who you are.

People who have been consistently mistreated by their parents do not know who they are. Let me say again that there are no perfect parents in the world anywhere. All parents have made some mistakes. So when I use the word "mistreated," I don't want us to automatically think of abuse. Someone speaking to you disrespectfully is mistreatment. Someone cussing at you is mistreatment. All mistreatment is wrong, but not all mistreatment is equal. The severity of the mistreatment determines whether it is abusive.

The greatest mistreatment our parents can do to us is failing to consistently define who we are. If parents do not "define" their children with consistent unconditional love, nourishment and nurture, those children will have a poor self-esteem. A poor self-esteem causes people to have either a low concept of themselves or an exalted concept of themselves. Both of these concepts are wrong. God did not create us to think too high or too low of ourselves. He created us to have a balanced view of ourselves. He created us to have good self-esteem.

Parents have a responsibility to define good self-esteem to their children. To have good self-esteem means to understand that one has strengths and weaknesses, to be positive about oneself, and to take care of oneself.

For children to have good self-esteem parents need to understand that their children have strengths and weaknesses as part of their personalities. Authoritarian parents and permissive parents tend to focus on one aspect of their children's personalities. Authoritarian parents focus on and seek to eliminate their child's weaknesses. Permissive parents focus on and seek to exalt their child's strengths. Parents must be balanced in their focus on their child's identity.

When Adam and Eve lost their pure connection to God, they lost their identity. They lost their balanced view of who they were. What Adam lost, Jesus restored (Rom. 5:17). Jesus restored our identity, yet if parents don't consistently define their children they can fall into the trap of a low self-esteem, "Yes, I am a worm," or the trap of an exalted self-concept, "No, I'm not a worm. You're a worm."

When we have good self-esteem we will be positive about ourselves and others. When we are not positive about others it is usually because we are not positive about ourselves. We have not taken care of ourselves. Joyce Meyers has often said that you can't give what you don't have. You must take care of yourself in order to help others. Taking care of yourself differs from being selfish in motive.

A person with good self-esteem will be motivated to maintain her personal life. In order to take care of herself she will maintain her spirit, soul and body. She will spend time with God; enjoy knowing the will of God and doing the will of God.

A selfish person or one with poor self-esteem is one who is motivated to protect himself. He is not always sure of what will happen to him. He does not spend time with God. He doesn't enjoy or do the will of God. He is confused.

As I have already covered, confused behavior comes from a spirit of rejection that parents have imparted to their children. Some parents send mixed messages to their children. On one hand they tell them how smart they are, but on the other hand they overreact to their children's weaknesses and call them "stupid." Some people are wasting their whole lives trying to figure out who they are. Are they smart or are they stupid?

Proverbs 22:1 says a good name is better than riches. Immediately, when you say a person's name an image comes with that name. By acting selfishly many people make a bad name for themselves. My name "Pamela" means honey. Honey is naturally sweet. Even though every time someone says my name they call me "naturally sweet," I don't always act like a sweet person. However, my overall reputation is that I am a sweet and sensitive person. When the Bible talks about a good name it is actually talking about a person's reputation. A good reputation is better than gold.

Many people dislike their natural name, but actually it is their reputation they are trying to overcome. I believe Jacob was that way. His name meant supplanter. Supplant means to take the place of; supersede, especially through force or plotting. Jacob's reputation was that he was a selfish man. He deceived his father to get his brother's blessing. The blessing was Jacob's. God had already chosen him (Gen. 21-23). But Jacob did not want to wait to receive it. He saw that his father was old and he took advantage of his father's age (Gen. 27:1-40).

Selfish people take advantage of other people. They may take advantage of someone's kindness. They may take advantage of someone's age. They may take advantage of a person's physical condition.

Still, when people attempt to get honor for themselves, their reputation will not be honorable. Their motives and their ways are ungodly. God says if you will give Me honor, I will give you honor (I Sam. 2:30). Honor is a gift that you should give your parents and a gift that you should give to God.

Honor Is a Gift

Most people equate honor with power. In Matthew, Mark and Luke there are accounts of the disciples arguing about who is the greatest (Matt. 18:1-4; Mark 9:33-37; Luke 9:46-48). Jesus tells them in each of the Gospels not to be concerned about who is the greatest. He says to be the servant of all. Then in the book of John Jesus actually washes the disciples' feet! This was so greatly unheard of that Peter said, "Not so, Lord. You will never wash my feet." Jesus told Peter unless He washed his feet he had no part in him. Peter did not understand the role of honor. They greatly honored Jesus. Jesus wanted honor, but He received it as a gift (Jn. 13:1-17). I want honor from my children, but I must receive honor from my children as a gift. I can't take it from them. I can't make them honor me because honor is a heart attitude. I can tell them when they are not honoring me, but honor only comes from the heart. Parents cannot make their children honor them. They can make their children obey, but they cannot make them give them honor. God says that children are to give it, but in order to give it the children must not have any resentment in their hearts against their parents.

Again, some parents will read this and say, "My children better honor me." You cannot take honor. You can only receive it. There are seasons when children will test you. They may be in a season of not honoring you. In this case you must wait for their hearts to change towards you. God has made a generational promise that if children honor their parents it will be well with them. If your child is not honoring you, stand on the promise that if you honor your parents then it will be well with you and believe that your children will obey the Word of God to honor you.

After all, God is the One who is giving you the honor. He said if you honor Him then He would honor you (I Sam. 2:30). He will cause your children to honor you if you wait for it. Impatience is the fruit of selfishness. Impatience is the result of taking honor rather than patiently receiving it. Impatience displeases the Lord.

For example, there are times when my son will chew his food with his mouth as open as he can without letting the food fall out of it. I know I can be very impatient with that behavior at that point and there will be consequences if he doesn't chew with his mouth closed. Well, in order for him to fully desire to change his behavior, he needs to understand that he is not honoring me. Yet I need to also realize that he is still very young. I have to patiently wait for him to consistently honor me. God is the God of order and timing. He has given me the ability to wait with a good attitude for my children to mature.

Parents Need a Good Attitude

Patience is a fruit of the Spirit. To have patience means one can wait…with a good attitude. All of us have to wait. Yet many of us do not wait with a good attitude. Many people do not wait for God to bring harmony in their families. They are frustrated. They are irritated. They have to wait, yet everyone around them knows that they are not satisfied waiting. They are not waiting with a good attitude.

Proverbs 14:14 says a good man will be satisfied with himself. Selfish people are always unsatisfied. Many people are dissatisfied with themselves and they take it out against their families. They will try to blame their family members for their dissatisfaction. It is my mother's fault. It is my father's fault. It is my husband or the kids' fault.

Apart from God a person will never be satisfied. Your spiritual thirst is what drives your thirstiness. Jesus said come to me all who are thirsty and I will give you drink (Jn. 7:37). You are the one who decides to drink. If you don't drink from the well that never runs dry, you will attempt to make people satisfy your thirst. They can't do it. Only God can give you the drink and only you can make the decision to drink. Your spouse can't make you drink. Your children can't make you drink. Your parents can't make you drink. You must decide you will drink. Jesus' invitation is to all who are thirsty.

Jesus says in Luke 12:15 to beware all kinds of greed. Thirsty people are greedy. People are thirsty because they believe that something other than God can make them content. Some people believe if they had more money they would be content. Some people believe that if they had a husband they would be content. Some people believe that if their parents had not mistreated them they would be content.

Those people believe that something "out there" will make them content. But Proverbs 23:7 says "as [a person] thinketh so is he." Your thinking determines whether you are going to be content or not. If you dwell on all the things you don't have, you will not be content. Paul said in whatever state I am in I have learned to be content; whether I am abundantly supplied with "it" or whether I have very little of "it" (Phil. 4:12).

It takes self-control to be content. It takes self-control to be patient. Many people will not be content without everything going their way. As I have mentioned earlier, people want power. They want to be in charge. So many teenagers say, "I can't wait 'til I'm on my own." It's natural for a teenager to want to grow up, but they still have to wait to be grown. I know when I was a teenager I was in a hurry to grow up, but as soon as I was on my own I missed Momma. I didn't miss her telling me what to do. But I missed her company. I realized when I got on my own that I really did love my mother. As I get older and my children are getting older, I can appreciate my mother much, much more. I have risen up to bless my mother (Prov. 31:28). One day your children will rise up to bless you. However, you must not under-use or overuse your authority over them.

God Is All Powerful

God has all the power, yet He has given authority to man (Rom. 13:1-2). However, God has not given every man equal authority. There are levels of authority in God's kingdom. We see it when Jethro instructed Moses to set up levels of authority (Ex. 18:17-26). We see Jesus being impressed with the centurion's faith because the centurion understood that there are levels of authority (Matt. 8:5-13).

God gave parents authority over their children until their children become adults (Eph. 6:1-3). God gave husbands authority over wives (Eph. 5:22-24). In order to walk in authority, we must walk in the boundaries God gave us. In order to walk unselfishly, we must walk in the boundaries God gave us. Many people do not handle being in charge well. They are too selfish. They are too busy thinking about what they want. They are not in charge to serve, but to be served.

You can tell if a person has a servant's heart simply by listening to him talk (Luke 6:45). You can tell by not only what he says, but also the way he says it. When people are sarcastic, they are acting selfishly. Sarcasm is taunting, sneering, cutting or caustic remarks. A sarcastic person is attempting to meet his need. Everyone has legitimate needs. However, when we try to meet our needs by belittling others we will do it selfishly.

God says He supplies all of our needs (Phil 4:19). When God told Abraham to sacrifice Isaac, Abraham took Isaac up to a mountain to sacrifice him. As they were going, Isaac, not realizing his father intended to sacrifice him, asked where the lamb was. Abraham told him God will provide Himself a lamb. Indeed, God provided a ram and Isaac was not sacrificed (Gen. 22:1-19). Abraham was fully convinced in God's ability to provide a lamb and deliver his son.

We display the most selfishness when we don't sacrifice the things God says to sacrifice. In First Samuel Chapter 15, Saul was instructed to destroy the Amalekites and everything they had. Saul told Samuel he did it when in fact he did not. Samuel knew Saul had not because he could hear the Amalekites' sheep bleating in the background. When God said "everything," He meant everything.

Saul gave an excuse for his partial obedience. He said the people wanted to save the best to sacrifice to the Lord. That sounds good. Doesn't it? God did say He does want us to sacrifice. However, total obedience to God is our best sacrifice.

In Abraham's and Saul's case, God showed He was interested in only one thing. Honor. Our obedience shows that we honor God. When we serve one another we honor God's Word (Gal. 5:13). God doesn't want a bunch of people who think they are #1. He wants people to show that He is #1. We display this by having an attitude to serve. "What can I do for you?" should be a common question on our lips. It should be a common question not only to our family members, but also to God. What is it that He wants us to do?

Thou Shalt Not Covet

God does not want us to be selfish. In the King James Version of the Bible, selfish ambition is translated covetousness and strife. Covetousness means wanting something someone else has while they still want it. You are not coveting something that someone has thrown away. Coveting means that person still wants it, but you want it from her.

When my son was about three he started coveting food. I had to be cautious not to tempt him if I had something I didn't want him to have. Other times, for example, he would touch my French fries and ask, "Can I have that?" Of course he could have it once he'd touched it. I have seen a wife ask her husband for the last bite of his dessert. He, being a little bit perturbed with her asking, said, "I already asked if you wanted some and you said no." She coveted his food.

Apart from being annoying, coveting can display serious emotional problems. A person who covets has a beggar mentality. If you have lived in any sizable city, you have seen a person on the street begging or crying out for money. A beggar basically covets your stuff. I understand that because of mental illness and financial hardship some people think they have to beg. But that is not God's best for them. God's best is that He would give them everything they need and that they should not have to beg man to supply their needs (Phil. 4:19).

Psalms 37:25 says the righteous are never forsaken and our children don't have to beg for bread. When you feel like someone in your family is begging or crying out, discern if they need love, nourishment or nurture. When you give your children love, nourish and nurture they will not feel the need to beg for what they need. They will be content.

There is an interesting point regarding coveting I must interject. There is a difference between someone coveting your "thing" and God telling you to give the "thing" away. Suppose your daughter wants a pair of earrings you own. And she asks, "Can I have these earrings, please?" Had God already spoken to you to give her those earrings? Some times we hold on to things too long because we really like them and do not really want to give them away. God is never trying to take something from you. He says to give and it will be given back to you. (Luke 6:38) As a parent, when you are generous with your children, generosity will come back to you from your children with honor.

The Servant of the Lord Must Not Strive

Instead of receiving honor from their children, many parents struggle with their children. Strife is the act of striving or trying very hard or struggling. God doesn't tell us to struggle to be who we are. We should not struggle with our relationships. Relating to our children isn't that hard. Relating to our parents isn't that hard. Relating to our spouses is not that hard. It is when we resist doing things God's way that our relationships are a struggle.

God had a plan for every family on this earth from the foundation of the world. Yet because many of us are impatient we do not realize God will fulfill His plan. Jacob was impatient. God had a plan for him from the foundation of the world. Yet when he selfishly stole his brother's blessing, he delayed the plan of God. God's plan is not for us to lie, cheat, or steal to fulfill His plan. The moment Jacob lied, cheated and stole, his life became a struggle. He had to run from his brother for his life (Gen. 27:41-44). He was deceived by his uncle into taking a wife he didn't want (Gen. 29:15-30). His uncle changed his wages ten times (Gen. 31:41).

Family problems. All the problems Jacob had stemmed from members of his own family. Yet because he was impatient he brought those problems on himself. God had a great plan for Jacob. The plan for Jacob was for him to become a community of peoples (Gen. 28:3). Still, not until Jacob decided to humble himself was he able to become more than a supplanter. After he humbled himself he became a prince. He became Israel (Gen. 32:28).

God has a great plan for you and me. The plan for you and me is that we become a community of peoples. Our humble attitudes will determine if we will be the best we can be. A selfish attitude prevents us from allowing God to show us who we are and what He created us to do. When we humble ourselves we will walk in the plan of God. Psalms 1:1-6 says:

> Blessed is the man that walketh not in the counsel of the ungodly, nor standeth in the way of sinners, nor sitteth in the seat of the scornful.
>
> But his delight is in the law of the LORD; and in his law doth he meditate day and night.
>
> And he shall be like a tree planted by the rivers of water, that bringeth forth his fruit in his season; his leaf also shall not wither; and whatsoever he doeth shall prosper.
>
> The ungodly are not so: but are like the chaff which the wind driveth away.
>
> Therefore the ungodly shall not stand in the judgment, nor sinners in the congregation of the righteous.
>
> For the LORD knoweth the way of the righteous: but the way of the ungodly shall perish. (KJV)

Humble Thyself

Humility is the way of the righteous. Humility gives us the ability to do what is right even when right things are not happening to us. A humble person will do what is right in God's sight (Jas. 4:10). Offenses come to give you an excuse to do what is wrong. When you are offended you have two options: act with humility or react with strife. When you act with humility you do not change your ways. You are still, in spite of the circumstances, going to do what the Word of God says. When you react with strife, you change.

You are not your real self when you strive with others. Your real self is who God made you to be. When God made you He did not make you a strife-filled person. He made you a happy person. He made you to have a smile on your face. He made you a loving, joyful, peaceful, patient, kind, good, faithful, humble person with self-control (Gal. 5:22-23).

Strife hinders who you are in Christ. Think about Lazarus. When Jesus called him out of the tomb he was still wrapped in burial clothes. Those clothes prevented him from walking freely. Those grave clothes had to come off in order for him to be himself again (Jn. 11:43-44). John 8:36 says, "Therefore if the Son makes you free, you shall be free indeed." Yet strife will prevent you from walking freely in His plan for your life.

God wants us to be free. He wants us to be free to serve Him. He wants us to be free to be the people He created us to be. He did not create us with grave clothes of strife. When Adam and Eve were formed they were naked and not ashamed. They were innocent. When they sinned they formed leaves to cover themselves. They had lost their innocence (Gen. 2:25).

When we were born we were so innocent. Babies are innocent. When we received Christ we became new creations (II Cor. 5:17). We became babes in Christ. Still, both naturally and spiritually, we lose some of our innocence when we strive against others.

Innocent means one is free from sin, evil or guilt; doing or thinking nothing morally wrong. To be innocent is to be pure. Children think wrong thoughts toward their parents when they strive with their parents. Until strife comes into the relationship children believe the best about their parents. When children strive with their parents they let go of their faith in their parents. When we as Christians strive with others we are thinking wrong thoughts. Until strife comes into our relationships with others we believe the best about them, and when Christians strive with others we are letting go of our child-like faith in God.

Second Timothy 2:24 says the servant of the Lord must not strive. Strife causes us to think negatively towards others. Children lose some of their innocence when they think negatively towards their parents. As Christians we lose our innocence when we think negatively toward others (Matt. 14:31). As Christians we lose our innocence when we refuse to walk in humility (Prov. 18:12).

Humility not Humiliation

Some people confuse humility with humiliation. Humility causes us to recognize our weaknesses. Humility will cause us to see that we don't have all the answers. Humility will cause us to acknowledge we need help. According to Webster's New World Dictionary, humiliation is the hurt of pride or dignity of by causing to be or seem foolish or contemptible.

Humiliation hurts pride (Prov. 29:23). God hates pride (Prov. 8:13). Humiliation often occurs when we act superiorly. When we think of ourselves more highly than we ought, God will allow us to see our utter weaknesses. He will let us fall on our face sometimes. He will let us see without His help that we can do nothing (Jn. 15:5). Humiliation often occurs when we don't humble ourselves.

Humble people recognize that they need help. Psalms 103:15 says that people are like grass. Our lives are like dust (Ps. 103:14). We are not self-contained entities. We are not self-made any things. Apart from God we can do nothing. Without God there is no strength. Without God we would have no hope. Do you realize you cannot live without hope? People commit suicide because they are hopeless. God is the God of all hope (Rom. 15:13). He gives us hope for better lives. He gives us hope to have better relationships. We need God. He sustains our very lives.

God's plan for you and me is to humble ourselves (II Chron. 34:27). Having an attitude of strife will prevent one from walking in an attitude of humility. Having an attitude of strife will cause someone to push against the plan of God. Have you ever noticed when you are vacuuming the carpet that if you vacuum with the pile the vacuum cleaner seems to glide by itself across the carpet, but when you vacuum against the pile the vacuum cleaner seems much more manual?

Strife causes relationships to be more manual. More effort. Harder to get along. When you don't demand your own way God will make the rough place smooth. He'll make the crooked places straight (Is. 45:2). When you demand your own way you push against others. When you are not humble God says you are wrong (Jas. 3:16).

Empathize With Others

An empathetic person is a humble person. What is your level of empathy? What is your level of really thinking about how others feel? When you empathize with others you try to feel what others are feeling. Before you speak or act you try to think about how that person will react. In role playing, you might think, "If I say this, he'll say that" or "If I do this, I know she'll be mad." But take it a step further. If you think, "If I say this, he'll say that," also think, "Why will he say that?" If you think, "If I do this, she'll be mad," also think, "Why will she be mad?"

When you don't empathize you may think "I know Mother won't like this, but I am going to do it anyway." When you don't empathize you don't mind hurting someone else just to get what you want. When you empathize with your family members, you will try to avoid making them feel bad. Feeling bad can mean feeling mad or sad. When we empathize we will not purposely make our family members feel bad. We will want to affirm them. We believe in them. We love them.

The Golden Rule is to do to others as you would have them do to you (Matt. 7:12). How would you feel if you were them? How would you feel if someone talked to you like that? How would you feel if someone treated you that way?

When you are empathetic towards your family members you show them your love. When you are empathetic towards your family members you will take the time to understand why they feel the way they do. When you are empathetic towards your family members you will consciously try to avoid hurting them.

There are times when we speak the truth in love to a family member and her feelings are hurt. God has called us to be honest people (Rom. 12:17). We are always to speak the truth to our family members. Though the truth hurts sometimes, our motive in speaking the truth should not be to hurt our family members.

When parents are not empathetic toward their children, they hurt their children's feelings. When your parents were not empathetic towards you and hurt you, forgive them. Jesus bore our pains and our weaknesses (Matt. 8:17). He is not a high priest that cannot be touched with the feeling of our infirmities (Heb. 4:15). He can help us forgive our parents for not empathizing with us. He cares about us. He cares about the "why" behind the way we feel. We should care about our families and the "why" behind the way they feel.

We do this most naturally with our children when they are babies. The baby is crying. Why is the baby crying? Is he wet? Is he hungry? Is he tired? When our children become old enough to talk we tend to be less patient in trying to understand why they are crying. We tend to be less empathetic. Consequently, as they get older they tend to cry less outwardly and more inwardly. When we can't see their tears many times we can't understand their behavior. When there is a communication breakdown there is strong potential for a break in the relationship.

In one great swoop, Jesus redeemed us from the curse of broken relationships (Gal. 3:13). Still, there is a process in enforcing His victory. The Bible says we go from faith to faith (Rom. 1:17). We usually don't get everything God has for us in one swoop. He is waiting for our faith to mature. He is waiting for us to humble ourselves. He is waiting for us to see how selfish we can be. If you don't stick with the process, you will not get the results you desire even though Jesus has already freed you from the curse of broken relationships. The good news is God is with you through the process (Matt. 1:23).

Here are a few godly ways to overcome selfishness:

1. First, acknowledge that you have been selfish. Most people want to feel that they are perfect. There are some people who truly are perfectionists. They believe they are the ones with all the wisdom, all the understanding and all the knowledge. There are extreme perfectionists and mild perfectionists, yet

Romans 3:23 says that we have all sinned. Jesus was the only perfect person who ever lived.

2. Secondly, repent. The Bible says that God looks after the humble in heart (Matt. 18:4). He knows where the dark spots of your heart are. He knows what causes you to grab instead of receive. He knows what causes you to be driven instead of led. Tell God you don't want to act that way any more and study humility.

3. Thirdly, maintain your spirit, soul and body (your self-esteem). Maintain your spirit by spending time in Bible reading and prayer. Maintain your soul by enjoying that you know the will of God. It is not enough just to know the will of God. You need to enjoy knowing it. And finally maintain your body. Your body is what carries out the will of God in your life.

4. Fourthly, be good to your family members. This will take some imagination. It would be easier to give a family member some money, but that family member would really appreciate the thought behind the "goodie." Your imagination is a powerful tool to use to express goodness to your family. Use your imagination to be a blessing to your family.

5. Fifthly, acknowledge all the good things that God does for you. He has blessed you with life and life more abundantly (Jn. 10:10). He has given you the keys to the kingdom (Matt. 16:19). He is on your side (Rom. 8:31-32) and He is working all things out for your good (Rom. 8:28).

The devil wants to use God's people to be instruments of unrighteousness. But we are the righteousness of God in Christ Jesus (II Cor. 5:21). We are vessels of honor (II Tim. 2:21). God will give us the strength to act like who we say we are.

God's Word on Knowing Who You Are:

In all things I am more than a conqueror. (Rom. 8:37)

Ye are the light of the world. (Matt. 5:14 KJV)

Know ye not your body is the temple of the Holy Spirit. (I Cor. 6:19 KJV)

Ye are of God, little children. (I Jn. 4:4 KJV)

Ridding Unrighteous Anger

Unrighteous anger is the emotion behind children dishonoring their parents. Unrighteous anger causes us to sin. The Bible is clear: Be angry, but sin not, don't let the sun go down on your wrath (Eph. 4:26). Anger is a righteous emotion. Still, just as too much of something good for you can turn into something bad for you, so it is with too much anger. It can lead you into sin.

Unrighteous anger is not only expressed as loud and rude. It is also expressed as quiet irritation, frustration, jealousy, fretfulness, or resentment. You have to know when you are angry in order to deal with your anger correctly. Until you can deal with your own anger correctly, you will never be able to teach your children how to deal with their anger. Unrighteous anger is then passed to the next generation who passes it to the next generation. The cycle of unrighteous anger in your family stops the flow of God in your family. When God is taken out of the equation, the blessing of God also stops flowing. The generational curse is then put in its place.

The purpose of anger can be legitimate, but our "just because we are mad" behavior will stop the flow of God's blessings in our families. Proverbs 14:29 says a quick-tempered man does foolish things. The devil is sneaky and he blinds people to the "foolish" things they are doing to cause the curse of disunity to be able to work in their family.

We can see the result of the curse working in our society. We can see divorce courts. We can see abortion clinics. The institutions of broken families are everywhere. They are the fruit of cursed people. Still the root of the curse is often hidden.

A fruit tree is easy to see. In our front yard, we have an apple tree. It is wonderful in the fall to see all those apples. That tree must have deep roots to support all of those apples. We have another tree that is beside our house. It too has deep hidden roots. But this shade tree is too close to the house and its roots caused the coupling on our water pipe to break. It was not wonderful to see all that water. Two trees. Two root systems. One a blessing. The other a curse.

There is a root assigned to every fruit of your spirit displayed. Unrighteous anger is a root of the generational curse of disunity.

Unrighteous anger is also a work of the flesh or the sinful nature of fallen man (Gal. 5:20). Cain was the first person in the Bible to use his anger to physically hurt someone. His wrath led to the first murder (Gen. 4:5-8). Cain had unrighteous anger. His actions showed that his heart was rooted in the curse of disunity. Your actions will reveal where your heart is really rooted.

Are You Seeking Justice?

As I have said before, anger is a legitimate emotion. Just as God gave humankind the emotions of happiness and sadness, He also gave us the emotion of anger. However, legitimate anger seeks a peaceful end.

Legitimate anger diffuses itself with godly wisdom, and godly wisdom that is from above, according to James, is peaceful (Jas. 3:17).

Anger is like a lawyer seeking justice. But if a lawyer breaks the law to get justice, he was not out for justice. He was out for revenge. He just wanted somebody to pay. This is the case with anger. If you are angry because you feel dishonored, and you seek a peaceful end, your anger has not been used to try to hurt anyone. But if you are angry because you feel dishonored and you verbally, emotionally or physically beat someone into submission to you, you were not really out for justice; you wanted revenge. You just wanted someone to pay. To make your family members pay for what they have done, have said, should have done, or should have said is unrighteous.

Revenge is at the heart of unrighteous anger. Revenge is weak man's attempt of self-protection. God said that vengeance was His (Heb. 10:30). He told us to love our brothers (I Jn. 5:11). He told us to pray for them (Jn. 17:9). It is hard to love and pray for someone you are holding a grudge against. So many adults, teenagers and even young children are acting out against their parents. They may be misbehaving at school, but the heart of the issue is they have a grudge against their parents. They may be stealing from the store, but the heart of the issue is they have a grudge against their parents. They may not be getting along with their spouse, but the heart of the issue is they never learned how to handle their anger against their parents.

Jesus said a prophet is without honor in his own home (Matt. 13:57). The same could be said for a parent. A parent can be successful in many different arenas, but not at home. Why is that? You have done your best. Many times you have sacrificed. Why is the parent without honor in his own home? After your children see your humanness or your weaknesses, they can become angry when you exert lordship over them. *How are you qualified to be lord over me?* they wonder. In Jesus' case, He is Lord of all (Rev. 17:14). He is qualified to be Lord. You, however, are a fallible and mistakable parent. Remember when you exert a lordship attitude over your children that you aren't qualified to be lord.

Jesus said the Gentiles seek to lord over others. This is not to be so with you (Matt. 20:25-27). God gave you the responsibility to love, nourish and nurture your children. This is not lording over them. This is serving them. When you try to lord over your children, they feel mistreated. When you condition your love, act selfishly toward, or use unrighteous anger against your children, they feel mistreated. They are mistreated.

The Curse Follows Dishonor

Many times children dishonor their parents because they feel mistreated, and just as it is natural for parents to feel angry when they are dishonored, so it is natural for children to feel angry when they are mistreated. When our children get angry with us and set themselves against us, they are sinning and setting themselves up for a cursed life. There are several scriptures that tell the outcome for children who curse or dishonor their parents.

- Exodus 21:15 – Anyone who attacks his father or his mother must be put to death.
- Exodus 21:17 – Anyone who curses his father or mother must be put to death.

- Leviticus 20:9 – If anyone curses his father or mother, he must be put to death. He has cursed his father or his mother, and his blood will be on his own head.
- Deuteronomy 21:18-21 – If a man has a stubborn and rebellious son who does not obey his father and mother and will not listen to them when they discipline him, his father and mother shall take hold of him and bring him to the elders at the gate of his town. They shall say to the elders, "This son of ours is stubborn and rebellious. He will not obey us. He is a profligate and a drunkard." Then all the men of his town shall stone him to death. You must purge the evil from among you. All Israel will hear of it and be afraid.
- Deuteronomy 27:16 – "Cursed is the man who dishonors his father or his mother." Then all the people shall say, "Amen."
- Proverbs 19:26 – He who robs his father and drives out his mother is a son who brings shame and disgrace.
- Proverbs 20:20 – If a man curses his father or mother, his lamp will be snuffed out in pitch darkness.
- Proverbs 28:24 – He who robs his father or mother and says, "It's not wrong" – he is partner to him who destroys.

The wages of sin are still death. When your children sin and dishonor you, they may or may not physically die for dishonoring you, but they will experience emotional death in their relationship with you and in other relationships. Your children may not understand what they are doing when they dishonor you, but you need to know what they are doing when they dishonor you. You need to know they are setting in motion the curse of disunity to play out in their lives.

The first place the curse of disunity starts is in the home with the father and the mother. For example, some parents may think it is so cute when the baby first starts talking and says 'no' to everything. Even when he says 'no' to his parents, it is so cute. But when that child is 15 or 16 years old that attitude will not be cute. That attitude will bring division in the relationship between that child and his parents.

There is no joy in having a cursed child. Today there are thousands of fathers and mothers weeping for their runaway children. Those children are living out the curse, but so are the parents. The Bible says when you are under the curse you will wear your eyes out looking for your children (Deut. 28:32). There are two faces of the curse. One side is your face and the other side is your child's face. One side is your reaction to your child and the other is your child's reaction to you.

Our Words Can Provoke Our Children

The Bible is very clear that children are to honor their parents. It is also very clear that parents are not to provoke their children to wrath (Eph. 6:4). Parents provoke their children's anger when parents don't discipline him correctly. Remember, parents must deal with the lie and the fear when disciplining their children. The generational curse is that the grandparents provoked the parents and the parents provoke their own children and so on and so on.

Parents also provoke their children by the way they talk to their children and the way they talk about their children. Proverbs 18:21 says that death and life are in the power of the tongue and those who love it will eat the fruit of it. You can tell the parents who purely love their children by how they describe them to you. You can also tell the parents who are provoking their children by how they describe them to you. Parents can kill their relationship with their children with their tongues.

Children are fragile. We tend to only see our children's fragility when they are babies or if they are sick. I believe the older they get the more you and I should remember that they are just dust (Ps. 103:14). Yet not only are children fragile, so are parents. Everyone is fragile. We are all dust. We were not made to take insults. We were not made to be belittled or ridiculed. We were not made to be rejected.

After many times of rejection, the heart becomes hard. As children we are born with soft hearts. Rejection makes the heart hard. To say to someone, "I don't love you any more," comes from a hard heart.

When questioning Jesus about divorce, some Pharisees asked him if divorce shouldn't be, then why did Moses tell the men to give their wives a written letter of divorce and send them away? Jesus said it is because of the hardness of their hearts (Matt. 19:3-8). Some people think divorce makes people hard hearted, but actually by the time the divorce comes the hearts have been hard for some time.

The Bible says out of the abundance of the heart the mouth speaks (Matt. 12:34). Listen to what the people around you are saying. When one has been cursed with disunity you will be able to hear the hardness of their hearts. The Bible says we bless and we curse out of the same mouth and this should not be. (Jas. 3:10) James 3:2 says when someone has control of their tongue they are a mature Christian. Does that mean a mature Christian will bless only? Is it possible to only bless our children? All things are possible to him who believes. (Mark 9:23)

Our Words Can Condemn Our Children

We should take control of our mouths. We should purpose to bless our children. Proverbs 15:1 says a gentle answer turns away wrath, but a harsh word stirs up anger. It seems the times I am most likely to speak harshly are when I am tired or ill. When you are tired or ill, remember the trap. The enemy wants to curse your children, but he needs your words. He needs you to say harsh words. He needs you to curse your children.

There are times I have made it a point to say to my children when they disappoint me, "I forgive you and there is no condemnation." Many people do not feel released from their sins, disappointing behaviors and failures. They carry the weight of condemnation into every relationship. Condemnation prevents people from accepting unity in their relationships.

If you responded in anger towards your parents or your children and you have not repented, you need to repent. The Holy Spirit is the one who convicts you of sin and will lead you to repentance. Many people confuse conviction with condemnation. When you read this book, don't feel condemned about mistakes you have made in the past or even today. The purpose of this book is not to make people feel condemnation or human sorrow (II Cor. 7:8-11). The purpose of this book is to allow the Holy Spirit to reveal to you why your relationships have not lasted and soften your heart so that you want your relationships to be meaningful and lasting (Ezek. 11:19).

Once you have repented for responding with unrighteous anger, there is no condemnation for you (Rom. 8:1). First of all, because everyone has responded with unrighteous anger at some point in their lives, no one can sit in judgment of you (Jn. 8:7). Secondly, if you have repented, you have no reason to be ashamed of yourself now for what you did in the past. I have used unrighteous anger against my family and I have felt the weight of condemnation about it. But I have chosen to release the weight of condemnation and walk in the freedom that Christ died for me to have (Gal. 5:1). I respond to the Holy Spirit when He convicts me of unrighteous anger. I repent and go on as if I had never sinned (Ps. 103:12). I walk in God's mercy (Ps. 52:8) and His forgiveness (Acts. 26:18).

Many people have been convicted, but did not repent. Instead they continued to display unrighteous anger until their family was destroyed. After their family has been destroyed then they feel bad about the things that they have done. Some of you reading this know that your anger destroyed your family. It is true you should be sorry for what you have done, but once you have repented, you have been cleansed from the guilt of all unrighteousness anger.

If you continue to allow condemnation to harass you, you do not believe that you have been forgiven and cleansed. Trust in the finished work of the cross. Jesus' blood cleanses all your guilty stains (I Jn. 1:7). When you are cleansed you don't want to respond with unrighteous anger. When you are cleansed you want to love, nourish and nurture your family.

God Wants to Prosper Your Family

Having a good relationship with your children is part of the generational blessing. Many times parents only believe that financial prosperity exemplifies that they are blessed. Abundant finances are part of being blessed (Prov. 10:22). Still, having a prosperous family is also part of being blessed (Gen. 12:2).

Many times money has the wrong place in people's hearts. They think their life would be blessed if they only had more money. Luke 12:15 says, "Beware of all kinds of greed." Possessing lots of money or not having a lot of money and wishing they had more money can make some people so greedy that they put their families in the wrong priority. Proverbs 15:27 says, "A greedy man brings trouble on his family." Your children are only going to be a certain age one time. When that time is spent, no matter how much money you have or don't have, you will never be able to get that time back. Jesus said in Matthew 6:25-33:

"Therefore I say to you, do not worry about your life, what you will eat or what you will drink; nor about your body, what you will put on. Is not life more than food and the body more than clothing? Look at the birds of the air, for they neither sow nor reap nor gather into barns; yet your heavenly Father feeds them. Are you not of more value than they? Which of you by worrying can add one cubit to his stature?

So why do you worry about clothing? Consider the lilies of the field, how they grow: they neither toil nor spin; and yet I say to you that even Solomon in all his glory was not arrayed like one of these. Now if God so clothes the grass of the field, which today is, and tomorrow is thrown into the oven, will He not much more clothe you, O you of little faith?

Therefore do not worry, saying, 'What shall we eat?' or 'What shall we drink?' or 'What shall we wear?' For after all these things the Gentiles seek. For your heavenly Father knows that you need all these things. But seek first the kingdom of God and His righteousness, and all these things shall be added to you."

God will take care of you (I Pet. 5:7). Fear not! (Is. 41:10). He promises that if you seek His kingdom first, He will provide every-thing you need (Matt. 6:33). Worrying about money will prevent you from seeking God's kingdom first (Matt. 13:22). Worrying about money will distort your relationship with your children. How? Why? The love of money is the root of all evil (I Tim. 6:10).

The love of your family is not the root of all evil. Some people believe they love their families so much. They think they would do anything for their family members. The proof will be in the question, "What about the money?" To many people the love of money is the root of the curse of disunity in their family. To some people money represents more than just being blessed to be a blessing. To some people money represents power. The Bible says how hard it is for rich people (and I might add, those who aren't rich, but want to be) to enter the kingdom of God (Matt. 19:23). Why? To them their money is their power source. To them their money is their god (Col. 3:5).

Let me reiterate, God wants us to prosper financially (III Jn. 2). However, He doesn't want us to prosper and lose our souls or our families (Matt. 16:26). Part of the curse is that your children will be taken from you and you will wear your eyes out looking for them (Deut. 28:32). If you haven't raised your children to be selfish, they don't care how much money you have. They care about how much you love them. I have watched my daughter, when she was two years old, being sweeter to a person who was almost homeless, obviously had nothing, and turn her face away from someone with a lot of money, who seemingly had everything. Life is not about the money (I Jn. 2:15-17). It is about relationships (I Jn. 2:9).

Purpose to Get Along

I can remember a time when I was young that I didn't want to live near my family. We were poorer than I thought we should have been and I felt I could make a better life for myself on my own. I had a superior attitude. I wanted to be independent. Little did I realize I was allowing the curse of disunity to work through my attitude. Hosea 4:6 says people perish for a lack of knowledge.

I thank God for my mother who purposed to get along with me. My life would have turned out so differently had she not persevered. Because of the children's lack of knowledge many of them are in a hurry to leave home. They can't wait to be 18. They can't wait to be on their own. Many parents allow their children to be on their own before those children are ready. Eighteen is not a magical number of maturation. Twenty-one is not a magical number of maturation. When "on your own" is fueled by the curse of disunity, those children are not ready to be on their own.

Families are supposed to grow into communities of peoples. If you look around the towns of America, you will see names like "Naperville" or "Warrenville." These towns were founded by one person who raised a family there and the family became a community of peoples.

Consider the Israelites. They are the sons and daughters of one man, Abraham. God told Abram that He would make him the father of many nations (Gen. 12:1). Abraham bore Isaac. Isaac bore Jacob. Isaac told his son Jacob that a community of peoples would come from him. (Gen. 28:3) Jacob passed on the knowledge of this purpose to his son, Joseph, saying, "A community of peoples shall come from you" (Gen. 48:4). When God delivered Israel out of bondage over a million people left Egypt (Ex. 12:37).

Some people moan when their family grows unexpectedly. But they should rejoice. Some people moan when it is time for the family reunion. But they should rejoice. God is in the business of growing and maintaining families. If you can't maintain good relationships with your family, the curse is working through you. To maintain means to keep or keep up; to keep or hold a place or position against attack; defend; to support by aid, influence and protection. It takes work to maintain a family. It takes an effort to get along. When you don't want to work at maintaining a good relationship with your family members, the curse of disunity is working through you.

Many people move away from their family members because they can't get along with them. There are times when a "time out" is needed. There are times when your family members are trying to hurt you. Still, many people are so sensitive to hurt feelings that they run even though no one is chasing them (Lev. 26:37).

Not everyone who moves away from their family feels chased. Some are breaking the curse. For many years I lived far from my parents and siblings. I am breaking the curse. I get along very well with everyone in my family. Abraham was told to move away from his family, to leave his father's house (Gen. 12:1). He was breaking the curse and establishing a new covenant. Missionaries are not living the curse. They are helping others to break the curse. When you want to leave your family because you do not get along with them you are living the curse.

When husbands and wives leave each other because life is not pleasant, the curse is at work in that family. When children want to leave home because they believe they can find a better life away from their family, the curse is at work in that family. When the curse has to be broken the children may need to go away; however, God's plan is that families get along and stay together.

The reason many children want to "go away" to college, as evidenced in the college students who go "wild" when they are away from home, is because they do not get along with their parents. One reason they do not get along with their parents is because they do not feel accepted by their parents. Many parents are unaware that their children feel unaccepted until it is too late to make any changes. A few years ago a college student, who was initiating into a fraternity at a university in Oklahoma, died from drinking excessive alcohol. His father said he didn't know his son drank. It is so sad that the parents were not aware that their son looking for acceptance before it was too late.

I want to encourage parents before it is too late to be aware of the desire of your children to have a "family" who accepts them. Many children find acceptance in their families, but others are still searching for it. Therefore, please know, if your children are or are not outwardly going against you, if you have been operating in any of the "cursed behaviors," your children still desire a "family" who will accept them. Without acceptance from you, their desire for acceptance can become too strong (or lustful – see Circle of Unity) and can cost them not only their sexual purity, but also their lives. It can change their destinies.

What is their destiny? Their destiny is that they get along with you. Their destiny is that they, along with you, become a community of peoples. Their destiny is that they achieve family unity.

What does family unity mean? It means more than to just go along with your parents. It means you know they accept and care about you, you accept and care about them and the members of the family live out the same godly principles. Psalm 133:1-3 says, "How good and pleasant it is for brethren to dwell in unity...for there the blessing flows." If you want family blessings, you have to purpose in your heart to maintain unity with your family.

You can get along with anybody who you want to get along with (Heb. 12:14). However, you have to decide to be a peacemaker (Matt. 5:9). You have to decide to love your family. You have to decide not to be selfish. You have to decide not to let your anger ruin your relationships.

Forgive Your Family Members

Unrighteous anger is the common symptom of disunity. When people are openly angry, they are not walking in love with their family members. Jesus told the parable of the unmerciful servant in Matthew 18:21-35.

Then Peter came to Jesus and asked, "Lord, how many times shall I forgive my brother when he sins against me? Up to seven times?"

Jesus answered, "I tell you, not seven times, but seventy-seven times."

Therefore, the kingdom of heaven is like a king who wanted to settle accounts with his servants. As he began the settlement, a man who owed him ten thousand talents was brought to him. Since he was not able to pay, the master ordered that he and his wife and his children and all that he had be sold to repay the debt.

The servant fell on his knees before him. "Be patient with me," he begged, "and I will pay back everything.' The servant's master took pity on him, canceled the debt and let him go.

But when that servant went out, he found one of his fellow servants who owed him a hundred denarii. He grabbed him and began to choke him. "Pay back what you owe me!" he demanded.

His fellow servant fell to his knees and begged him, "Be patient with me, and I will pay you back.

But he refused. Instead, he went off and had the man thrown into prison until he could pay the debt. When the other servants saw what had happened, they were greatly distressed and went and told their master everything that had happened.

Then the master called the servant in. "You wicked servant," he said, "I canceled all that debt of yours because you begged me to. Shouldn't you have had mercy on your fellow servant just as I had on you?" In his anger his master turned him over to the jailers to be tortured, until he should pay back all he owed.

This is how my heavenly Father will treat each of you unless you forgive your brother from your heart."

Sin Destroys Families

Unforgiveness is sin (Matt. 11:26). Sin is at the root of people who do not live in unity (Prov. 13:10). Sin causes us to think only of ourselves. God commands us to love one another (I Jn. 3:11). Love is what holds together our ability to walk in unity (Col. 3:14). When we walk in the love of God, sin is not encroaching at our door as it was with Cain (I Jn. 4:21). When the sinful nature is not motivating our behavior, we live in unity with the people around our lives.

Perpetual anger or bitterness is sin and destroys families. A bitter person tries to gain justice her way instead of God's way (Prov. 29:22). God is the God of order (I Cor. 14:40). He expects us to follow the chain of command (Eph. 5:22; 6:1). If young children are leading the family, how far can that family really go? How far will those children really go? They are out of the will of God.

How far can someone go who is out of the will of God? We can look at the life of Saul, Israel's first king. He had great potential, but he got out of the will of God (I Sam. 15:26). Though he continued to be king, God chose David to take his place (I Sam. 16:13). Queen Vashti got out of the will of God and she was replaced on the throne by Esther (Esther 1:12, 2:17). Jesus said a house divided cannot stand (Matt. 12:25). None of us can live in the blessings of God if we are not in the will of God.

God's plan is that we always live in His blessings. However, when we express "the wrath of man" we are out of the will of God

(Jas. 1:20). The wrath of man is an unrighteous expression of anger and it is out of the will of God. Sin and unrighteous anger go hand in hand. To sin means to miss the mark. Romans 3:23 says that all have sinned and have fallen short of the glory of God.

Sin is a very serious thing with God. In the Old Testament, every time someone sinned an animal had to die in their place (Lev. 5:5-6). What if your ministerial job was to slaughter the animals for the peoples' sins? You would have job security. Still, because we no longer sacrifice animals for our sins, we can think too lightly about our sins. Sometimes we believe we are getting away with something. Yet when God says the wages of sin is death, he was not saying that as an idle threat (Rom. 6:23).

Jesus died because of our sins. The light really came on for me the day I realized that every time I had a fit of anger that was the very reason Jesus had to die. So every time you mishandle your anger (quiet or loud) think of Jesus suffocating, asphyxiating, unable to breathe, on the cross…because of that.

It was a revolutionary thought to the people in Jesus' day when he said he would die one time for everyone's sins. The Jewish custom of animal sacrifice was that the death of an animal happened every time a person sinned. But as Paul said, "For just as through the disobedience of the one man the many were made sinners, so also through the obedience of one man the many will be made righteous" (Rom. 5:19).

Are You Carrying Your Cross?

Jesus has made us righteous. Still He did not want to go through the pain and suffering of the cross. Many people don't mind dying for a cause, but nobody wants to suffer. Jesus suffered before He went on the cross knowing that He would die a suffering death. He earnestly prayed three times that if it were possible that God should take this cup away from Him (Matt. 26:36-44). Yet he **knew** he was the lamb to take away the sins of the whole world – once and for all (Jn. 1:29). I emphasize "knew" because many people do not know the purpose for their family so they won't suffer on behalf of them.

Jesus was willing to suffer for us. He did not defend himself (Is. 53:7). When it was time for Jesus to be arrested, he said in Mark 14:48-50, "'Am I leading a rebellion that you come out with swords and clubs to capture me? Every day I was with you, teaching in the temple courts, and you did not arrest me. But the Scriptures must be fulfilled.' Then **everyone** deserted Him and fled." It wasn't until that moment that the disciples understood that Jesus wasn't leading a rebellion. It was until that moment that they were waiting and hoping to participate in the liberation of Israel from the Roman government (Mark 11:9-10). They said they wanted the kingdom of God, but more so they wanted to be free from Roman rule. They wanted to lead a rebellion.

There are many rebellious Christians. There are many Christians who will defend themselves to the bitter end. They don't realize that God isn't leading a rebellion. As children many of us acted rebelliously. We used defensive mechanisms against our parents. A defense mechanism is something you do to avoid being emotionally or physically hurt. You cover your ears to prevent hearing someone correct you. You put your hand up to prevent being spanked. As children we thought we were defending ourselves from our mean old parents, but Jesus said we only were rebelling against our parents (Matt. 10:21). We only wanted to be free from parental rule.

Just as the disciples did not understand the kingdom of God, many Christians do not understand the kingdom of God (Luke 17:20-21). The Bible says "we are considered as sheep to be slaughtered" (Rom. 8:36). Do you know that sheep have no defense mechanism? They are gentle, peaceful, unsuspicious animals. They allow themselves to be slaughtered. In order to overcome unrighteous anger we must allow ourselves to be "slaughtered."

We may have to "suffer" to get along with our family members. Jesus gave us the example to follow. Therefore, we must follow Jesus' example of when He was falsely accused. We must follow Jesus' example of when he was unjustly treated. We must follow Jesus' example of when he was dishonored. We must deny our right to defend ourselves, take up our cross and follow Him (Matt. 16:24).

Jesus could have really made ruling authorities sorry for what they had done. He could have really made them pay for what they had done, but He didn't (Matt. 26:52-53; Jn. 19:11). He forgave them (Luke 23:34). His life purpose was to give His life away (Gal. 1:4). Jesus knew His purpose. He knew He was the only way for us to overcome sin and unrighteous anger. He knew He was the only way to the Father (Jn. 14:6). He knew He was the only way to eternal life (Jn. 3:16).

<u>You Can Change</u>

Once we were blind to our behavior or powerless to change. Change is not easy. Still, Christ has given us His resurrection power not only so that we can see our destructive behavior, but also to overcome sin and unrighteous anger (Rom. 6:9). When we have Christ, we have the same power that caused Him to rise from the dead (Rom. 8:11). That is power!

God has given us the power to change our cursed behaviors (Phil 4:13). Through His power we can overcome the generational curse of disunity in our families. Through His power, we can overcome unrighteous anger. Through His power, we can change.

Here are a few godly ways to deal with anger.

1. When you feel angry, stop before acting or talking. It has been noted that we have one mouth and two ears. Do not be quick to speak and do not become quick to become angry (Jas. 1:9).
2. Ask yourself if this is righteous anger. If it isn't, then you simply need to let it go. If it is, consider the source of the accusation, mistreatment, or dishonor. Is your child dishonoring you? Is your spouse dishonoring you? Is your parent dishonoring you? The source of the dishonor will determine how you are to respond.
3. Pre-determine how you will respond to dishonor. Pre-determine the response based on the source. How will you respond if it is your child? How will you respond if it is your spouse? How will you respond if it is your parent?

4. Make a decision to always respond with love (value + positive treatment). When you respond with love, you will not respond with revenge. When you respond with love, you will truly seek godly resolutions. When you respond with love, you will truly prove you care about your family and want unity with them.
5. Make it a habit to repent when you respond with unrighteous anger. God will forgive you. Your family will forgive you. And you can forgive yourself.

Anger measures dishonor and unfair treatment. Your anger is a meter to determine if you or others are being treated unfairly. Your reaction to your anger determines if you are going to treat others unfairly. Does unfair treatment stop with you? Or will you continue the cycle?

You are responsible for how you react. No one else is. You control your reactions. No one else does. You allow yourself to get angry. No one else makes you mad. You have self-control (Gal. 5:22). Therefore, you control your temper. You control your peace.

God's Word on Living without Unrighteous Anger:

Be not hasty to be angry. (Eccl. 7:9 KJV)

Let all anger be put away. (Eph. 4:31)

Great peace have they who love your law, and nothing can make them stumble. (Ps. 119:165)

We have peace with God through Jesus Christ. (Rom. 5:1)

Section Three

Stay on the wall… (Neh. 4:17)

Embracing the Generational Blessing

The generational blessing is unity in your family. Nehemiah 4:17 encourages the people to stay focused on the rebuilding of the walls of Jerusalem. Once the walls were rebuilt, the inhabitants had greater security and as a consequence, the flow of blessings in their lives. Just as Nehemiah 4:17 was a word to people rebuilding their lives, it is also a word to parents to stay focused on maintaining or rebuilding unity in their families. It is also a word that God will bless our families as we obey Him.

Before the fall, Adam and Eve had the blessing of God. They were in unity and were blessed with everything they needed. According to Nelson's Illustrated Bible Dictionary, blessing is "the act of declaring... God's favor and goodness upon others. The blessing is not only the good effect of words; it also has the power to bring them to pass." God will abundantly bless us when all of our family members are doing what He says to do. We will receive the curses if we disobey God (Deut. 28:15-68). We have already seen what the curses detail. Let's take a look at the blessings listed in Deuteronomy 28:1-14 (NLT). I have highlighted the parts of the blessing that pertain to the family.

> **"If you fully obey the LORD your God by keeping all the commands I am giving you today, the LORD your God will exalt you above all the nations (families) of the world.**

2 You will experience all these blessings if you obey the
LORD your God:

3 You will be blessed in your towns and in the country.

4 **You will be blessed with many children** and produc-
tive fields. You will be blessed with fertile herds and
flocks.

5 You will be blessed with baskets overflowing with fruit,
and with kneading bowls filled with bread.

6 You will be blessed wherever you go, both in coming and
in going.

7 "The LORD will conquer your enemies when they attack
you. They will attack you from one direction, but
they will scatter from you in seven!

8 "The LORD will bless everything you do and will fill your
storehouses with grain. The LORD your God will
bless you in the land he is giving you.

9 **"If you obey the commands of the LORD your God and
walk in his ways, the LORD will establish you as
his holy people as he solemnly promised to do.**

10 **Then all the nations (families) of the world will see
that you are a people claimed by the LORD, and
they will stand in awe of you.**

11 **"The LORD will give you an abundance of good
things in the land he swore to give your ancestors
— many children, numerous livestock, and abundant crops.**

12 **The LORD will send rain at the proper time from his
rich treasury in the heavens to bless all the work
you do. You will lend to many nations (families),
but you will never need to borrow from them.**

13 If you listen to these commands of the LORD your God
and carefully obey them, the LORD will make you
the head and not the tail, and you will always have
the upper hand.

14 You must not turn away from any of the commands I
am giving you today to follow after other gods and
worship them.

Doesn't being blessed sound good? Isn't that a good plan for your family? There are no bad or sad happenings associated with being blessed. However, the blessings do not flow where God's commands are not carried out and the blessings do not flow where there is no unity. You may say, "I know people who argue a lot and have a lot of money. They are not carrying out God's commands yet still appear to be blessed." Proverbs 10:22 says the blessing of the Lord maketh rich and He adds no sorrow with it. Be not deceived. There is sorrow for families who do not walk in unity.

A generational blessing occurs when the parents obey God, the children obey God, and the grandchildren obey God. And the good news is that as the generations obey God the blessing is firmly established in a family. Psalm 133:1-3 depicts how God thinks unity should look in a family.

> How good and pleasant it is when the brethren dwell in unity.
> It is like precious oil poured on the head, running down the beard, running down on Aaron's beard, down upon the collar of his robes.
> It is as if the dew on Hermon were falling on Mount Zion. For there the Lord commanded the blessing, even life for evermore.

As we read this verse, we see the precious oil running down Aaron's beard and as if the dew on Mount Hermon was falling on Mount Zion. Aren't those sweet pictures? Doesn't the picture of ease fill your mind? Doesn't a calm feeling fill your heart?

Two concepts stick out to me about the picture of unity that God has given us. One is there is a flow. Did you notice that the oil was not stopped? Did you notice that the dew continued to fall? There should be a flow to your family's lifestyle. Many families are in such upheavals. They move a lot. They stop and start relationships often. They never really establish any roots. There is not a continual flow.

The other concept that sticks out to me is the authority of the examples. Aaron represents the head of the priestly family and

Mount Hermon is a big mountain. Mount Zion is a mountain smaller than Mount Hermon. Unity has to flow from the people in authority. Unity has to flow from the "big people" to the "little people." Parents are the ones to establish unity in their families.

To God unity among family members is very precious. Unity is the key to receiving the blessing of God. Unity is the key for those blessings to flow through generation to generation. If your parents have taught you how to be unified, you have received a blessing that money cannot buy.

Family unity occurs when family members really get along. Family unity is not sameness. It is unique family members living in harmony for a common goal, something we want to accomplish. The day-to-day goals may change, but the ultimate goal of family unity is that our family get along with God and accomplish His plan for our lives (Num. 18:2, II Chron. 20:13).

Family unity means the people in the family agree with each other more often than they disagree with one another. There is power in agreement. When we understand how great the power of agreement is we will do everything in our power to maintain unity in our families. Genesis 11:1-9 (KJV) says:

> And the whole earth was of one language, and of one speech.
>
> And it came to pass, as they journeyed from the east, that they found a plain in the land of Shinar; and they dwelt there.
>
> And they said one to another, Go to, let us make brick, and burn them thoroughly. And they had brick for stone, and slime had they for mortar.
>
> And they said, Go to, let us build us a city and a tower, whose top may reach unto heaven; and let us make us a name, lest we be scattered abroad upon the face of the whole earth.
>
> And the Lord came down to see the city and the tower, which the children of men builded.
>
> **And the Lord said, Behold, the people is one, and they have all one language; and this they begin to do: and now**

nothing will be restrained from them, which they have imagined to do.

Go to, let us go down, and confound their language, that they may not understand one another's speech.

So the Lord scattered them abroad from thence upon the face of all the earth: and they left off to build the city.

Therefore is the name of it called Babel; because the Lord did there confound the language of all the earth: and thence did the Lord scatter them abroad upon the face of all the earth.

<u>There Is Power in Agreement</u>

Can you see the power that is available to people who will agree? God said that when these people had one mind nothing would be impossible to them. Although the tower of Babel is a negative example of agreement, the first point I want to bring out about this passage of scripture is in order to accomplish great things, you and your family members must agree. You must agree about what you are doing and where you are going as a family. The second point about this passage is to keep from being scattered your agreement has to be in line with the will of God.

You and your family members cannot agree about anything outside of God's will and expect it to come to pass. God does not honor things done disorderly. Ananias and Sapphira were a married couple who agreed to lie to the apostle Peter about some money they had acquired. They had no reason to lie. They gained no advantage for lying. As I have said before, lying gives no one advantage. The result of Ananias' and Sapphira's agreement was they both died early deaths (Acts 5:3-10). Obviously, God did not put lying in Ananias' and Sapphira's heart. Jesus said if any two on the earth shall agree about anything **that God** has put in their heart, God will grant them to have what they agreed on (Matt. 18:19).

Before people marry they should find out what the two of them agree on. A lot of people marry on assumption. When Otha and I married I assumed we would agree on how to spend the money, but after we married I was so concerned that we would not agree that I wanted separate checking accounts. As my husband and I were not in agreement about money, we were consistently finding ourselves with financial shortages.

Financial disunity was one of the attitudes that I carried from my mother's house to my marriage. I didn't agree with my mother about how to spend money and when I got married I didn't agree with my husband on how to spend money. The attitudes that we carry toward our parents will impact every relationship that we have, especially in the areas of authority.

I have said it a lot, because I want you to believe it... God has a good plan for your life. In order to receive it, you must live in unity with your family members, the primary members being your father and mother. In Leviticus 20:12 God tells us that if we honor our father and mother then it will be well with us. Wellness is a state of mind. When you honor your father and mother you will have a well mind. You will have a peaceful mind. You will have a sound mind. In Second Timothy 1:7 Paul says God has not given us the spirit of fear, but of love, power and a sound mind.

When you honor your father and mother you will have an agreeable spirit. That doesn't mean we will always like what our parents say or do, but it does mean that we will always keep an agreeable attitude. An agreeable attitude is to have an attitude of always giving your parents the benefit of the doubt. There are disagreements in every family, but when you have a general attitude of agreement, disagreements will be much easier to resolve and the level of distrust will be down.

Parents Do Have Wisdom

As I have said before, people who trust have better relationships. People who trust their parents will have better relationships. People who trust God will have better relationships.

Trust can be given to parents even though they may not be perfect. Again, there are no perfect parents, but God is perfect. When you honor His Word, He will honor you. God will honor you for honoring your parents. At the same time that good things are happening to us because we honor our parents, bad things are not happening to us for the very same reason. That means there will be a lot of trouble we avoid because we honor our parents. We will walk in blessings and not curses if we honor our parents.

Again, this does not mean there will not be any disagreements. There will be disagreements. Your parents have one mind and you have another mind. In family unity there is plenty of room for a person's uniqueness. Still, as it says over and over in Proverbs, listen to your parents (Prov. 1:8, 4:1, 5:1, 7:1). Remember God has a chain of command.

As adult children we are still to honor our parents. You may think once you grew up you no longer had to listen to your parents. The truth is the commandment to honor your father and mother is not written just for young children, but adults as well. Notice Leviticus 20:12 does not say "Obey your father and mother and it will be well with you." Honor does not mean obey. It means respect. Honor is an attitude of mind that plays out through action. Respect your father and mother and it will be well with you. However, when your child respects you, a young child will obey you. When your adult child respects you, he will value your opinion.

To a young child and even a teenager, parents are their world. Because their experiences are so limited in life, they need us in every way. Parents provide food, clothes, and money for their children's education. Parents provide for their fun. Parents' opinions are priceless. Nevertheless, as the children grow up, parents are to give their opinion less and less. Children need fewer and fewer commands as they mature. Children need to be able to make more and more of their own decisions so that one day they will be able to stand on their own.

As adults we seek advice, not commands. Commands we can get from the Bible (Jn. 12:50). This is not to say that if your parents tell you to do something, who to marry, or what to wear that you would ignore them. In fact, when your parent "commands" you about something, you should take that very seriously. Weigh what they are saying. But the final decision belongs to you.

I remember when I had my son, my firstborn, in the delivery room my mother told me to push. She didn't ask me to push. She didn't suggest that I push. She said, "Pam, push." There was a seriousness that came with those words. I agreed with her and pushed. Moments later Andrew Joseph Ellis was born, weighing 6 lbs. 5 oz. I could have ignored her. I could have disagreed, but I listened to her. I trust my mother.

If your parents have not overcome generational curses of disunity, you will need to resist the curse when it comes through them (Ps. 27:10). When your parents do things to confuse you, act selfishly or respond in anger towards you, you must resist the curse by resisting the urge to respond with confusion, anger or selfishness.

Recently, I wanted to do something I knew my mother would not like. I told her about it and she didn't want me to do it. But this was something I felt very strongly about. I felt God was motivating me to do it. I had agreement with my husband. So I would not be dissuaded. Still, I talked to her about her concerns because she was indirectly involved and I wanted her to unite with me. Also, I respect my mother's opinions. I trust her. She is a very strong Christian and I wanted her prayers. What I was doing was going to be difficult, but it could be done and it could be done with ease if everyone involved, directly and indirectly, was in agreement.

As I talked to her I sensed that fear was behind why she didn't want me to do it. I denied fear a place. Ephesians 4:27 says to give the devil no place. The devil is the one who wants us to be afraid. Mother overcame that fear. She was able to stay in faith. She agreed with me and God cleared the way. Everything went well. Again, wellness is a state of mind that is formed through the attitude of honor. I could have ignored Mother's concerns, but in order to honor her I could not ignore her concerns. I had to address her concerns.

I honored my mother, but I did not honor the fear. Fear is part of the curse. When we realize the root of our parents' concerns we can talk with them as adult-to-adult instead of child-to-adult. Jesus said we would have trouble or disagreements, but the blessing is that we will overcome them all (Jn. 16:33). We will overcome them all if we have a well mind. Jesus said to those that overcome He will give the crown of life (Rev. 2:7).

You Can Trust God

Those who overcome disunity will also receive supernatural deliverance. They will receive supernatural breakthroughs. Before the Israelites left Egypt the Bible says that they all obeyed when Moses told them to put the blood of the lamb on the doorposts (Ex.12:21-28). *All* is a powerful word. That means there was no one who didn't do it. There was no one who only put the blood on one doorpost instead of all three. There were no exceptions. They all carried out all of the instructions God commanded them to do through Moses. When they all had done it the destroyer was not able to harm any of their families. They were all supernaturally delivered from Egyptian rule (Ex. 12:29-42).

In every area of your life you need to agree with your family members to do what is right. Unity will cause you and your family members to agree about how to spend money so that you and your family members will be blessed with financial increase. Unity will cause you and your family members to agree that healing is for today so that you and your family members will maintain good health. Unity will cause you and your mate to agree about how to discipline your children and your children will grow up to be a blessing to you, your spouse, their spouses, their children and God.

In His Word, God has provided everything that we would ever need. He has provided everything pertaining to life and godliness (II Pet. 1:3). He has provided bread to the eater and seed to the sower (Is. 55:10). He has provided household salvation through His Son Jesus (Acts 16:31, 34). When we accept Jesus there is nothing that we need that God doesn't provide. We are a blessed people through our unity with Jesus Christ (II Cor. 1:20).

Through His Word, God has provided unconditional love and training in righteousness. He sets a table before us in the presence of our enemies (Ps. 23:5). God is a good God. He is also the world's greatest Dad. He is our example for parenting. The Bible says if we who are evil know how to give good gifts to our children, how much more does God the creator of all life know how to give us good things? (Matt. 7:11). When we obey His Word, we will walk in the blessings of unity. Family unity consists of loving, nurturing and nourishing our family members.

Loneliness, physical sickness, poverty and disobedient children are not part of the blessing. Disunity, confusing behaviors, selfish ambition and unrighteous anger are not part of the blessing. If you are walking in any of these areas, please understand that these attitudes and problems are not God's will for your life. God's will is for us to be blessed.

Some people think because they are a good person they should be blessed. God does not want us to be deceived about our "goodness." If you thought you were a good child, but you were consistently disobedient towards your parents, you were not a blessing to your parents. That does not mean as a child you could never make mistakes. Children are children. They are going to make mistakes. However, for a child to be a blessing, he attempts to honor his parents.

As Christians one of our goals in life is to be a blessing. When I sent my five-year-old son off to school I would remind him to be a blessing. Being a blessing has the same meaning of being good, but with the added understanding of purposely being good to someone. Many times when we tell our children to be good we mean that they shouldn't be bad. Being a blessing is more than not being bad. Being a blessing means being good to someone on purpose.

Our Children Are Blessed

The entire premise of my writing this book is my belief that in order to have blessed relationships with others we must have a blessed relationship with our parents. If you fought against your parents as a child, if you are fighting against your parents as an adult, if your children are fighting against you, now is the time for the fighting to stop. Now is the time to believe your parents are a blessing so that you can clearly see *how* you can have a blessed relationship with your children.

The Bible says we will be blessed in the fruit of our womb (Deut. 28:4). The fruit of the womb is our children. God says our children will be blessed. Still, how we treat our children will determine if they walk in the blessing of God. If we believe they are a blessing, they will be blessed everywhere they go. If we believe they are a burden, they will be a burden everywhere they go. Even parents who are not abusive can still hold the attitude that their children are a burden instead of a blessing.

The attitude of the parent toward their child will determine what kind of care their child will receive. This does not justify mistreatment of any child. But it does denote one reason why some innocent children receive bad treatment. If you take your child to a daycare or school and those teachers or administrators do not recognize your child as a blessing, you should have a serious talk with that teacher or administrator while looking for a daycare or school that values all children.

The Bible says that children are a heritage (Ps. 127:3). Some people are only living for today, but our children are the future of this country and even the world. Even if your parents did not receive you as a blessing, if you honor them, you will recognize your children as a blessing. Many people only see the big house, the big car, degrees behind their name as the blessing. Consequently, many times when they get material fortune and fame they lose their families.

I am not against people who gain fortune and fame. God wants good things for us and He wants us to have the good desires of our hearts. Nevertheless, He wants one of our top desires to be united with our families.

In order to walk in unity we must have prosperous souls. When we have prosperous souls we will see the value in our family members. When we have prosperous souls we will recognize our parents, ourselves, and our children as gifts. If you have received Jesus as your Savior, then you know by the price that He paid for you that you are valuable. He also paid a great price for your family members. They also are valuable. He paid a great price for you and your family members to have blessed lives (Acts 16:31).

God's Word Does Not Change

God puts family members together (Ps. 68:6). He put the generations together. He knew what family you should grow up in because

He knew what kind of world you would live in. God is the God of every generation. The life your parents lived is not the same life you will live, and the kind of life your children will live will not be the same life that you lived. Times change, but Jesus said He was the same yesterday, today and forever (Heb. 13:8). His Word will stand forever (Prov. 19:21).

Isaiah 54:13 says all of my children shall be taught of the Lord and great shall be their peace. Ephesians 6:4 says that parents are not to provoke their children, but bring them up in the training and instruction of the Lord. Some people seem to be wonderful with children and I don't mean overly permissive.

Some parents seem to know intuitively how to love, nourish and nurture their children. But if you talk to them you find out it is a learned behavior. They were taught to be that way. My sister-in-law made a point about this. As she and I were driving in her car one day she told me she often felt inferior as a mother because she didn't know some of the "common sense" things about child rearing. Her mother died before she had children; therefore, when she had a child her mother was not there to teach her some of the "common sense" things about child rearing.

Walking in family unity has to be taught. It has to be explained and modeled. The unity principles are love, nourish and nurture. We must love our children while teaching them to love others in order for our families to walk in unity (Titus 2:3-4). We must nourish our families while teaching them to nourish others in order to walk in unity (Jn. 21:15-17). We must nurture our families while teaching them to nurture others in order for families to walk in unity (Prov. 22:6).

Blessed People Are Thankful

When our families walk in unity we are truly blessed people. When our families walk in unity we are truly thankful people. We are not only to bless our children, but to teach them to be thankful for their blessings. Blessings come from God. When our children can recognize blessings they should also be taught to bless God. The

Psalmist said, "I will bless the Lord at all times. His praises shall be continually in my mouth" (Ps. 34:1).

Everyone should praise God. He has done so much for us. We are blessed with health. We are blessed with a nice place to live. We are blessed with wonderful families. One of the first prayers we taught our children is a mealtime blessing. Here is a mealtime prayer that my children say:

Thank You, God
For this food
Make it nourishment
For my body,
In Jesus' Name. Amen.

Very young children can say "thank you," and a child as young as 18 months or even younger (for more verbal children) can easily recite this prayer. God said He chose Abraham because Abraham would teach his children about God (Gen. 18:19). God told David that He would keep David's descendants on the throne if they continued to follow Him (I Kings 2:4). God chose you as a parent with the purpose that you would teach your children about Him. When we teach our children to honor us, we are teaching them to honor God. Those that honor God, He will honor them with a blessed life (I Sam. 2:30).

Here is how to biblically walk in unity with others:

1. Love your family members unconditionally. Give them room to grow and make mistakes. Do things together that are fun. Children want fun. They want a lot of opportunities to laugh and giggle. Provide an atmosphere where it is not always business as usual.
2. Nurture and train them to honor you. As you train your children to honor you, train them to pray. God is the strength of our lives (Ps. 27:1). God is the one who is going to cause your family to walk in unity. Ask Him to help your family.
3. Nourish their bodies and souls. A good meal for the stomach and good encouragement for the soul helps keep families

together. Be interested in what the other members of the family are doing. Be supportive and attentive. Be available to attend games or performances. Time spent with your family is time well spent.

The Bible says do everything in the bond of unity which is love (Col. 3:14). Love is the bond of unity. Love is what holds it all together. The next chapter is about love. It is what the world needs. It is what your family needs. It is what you need.

God's Word on Unity:

For [God] hath strengthened the bars of your gates; He hath blessed your children within you. (Ps. 147:13 KJV)

[My] seed shall be mighty upon the earth: the generation of the upright shall be blessed. (Ps. 112:2 KJV)

For I will pour water on the thirsty land, and streams on the dry ground. I will pour out My Spirit on your offspring, and my blessing on your descendants. (Is. 44:3)

The Lord will increase you more and more, you and your children. (Ps. 115:14 KJV)

Loving Your Family

God is funny about motivations. I don't mean "ha-ha" funny. I mean that He is very particular about how people are to be motivated. He wants us to be motivated with a pure heart. In Proverbs 4:23 God tells us to guard our hearts with all diligence for out of it flows the issues of life. God tells us in First Samuel 16:7 that He doesn't look on outward appearances, but He looks at the heart. God is watching out for our heart responses to life.

For the eyes of the Lord run to and fro throughout the whole earth, to show himself strong in the behalf of those whose heart is perfect toward Him (II Chr. 16:9). Having a perfect heart does not mean that you don't ever make mistakes. In fact, you don't have a perfect heart if you think that you are always right and don't ever make mistakes. You are in pride if you believe that you don't make mistakes and God hates pride (Prov. 8:13). When He says He is looking for people who have a perfect heart, He does not mean someone who is perfect. He means someone who is fully committed or sensitive to Him.

God is a Spirit (Jn. 4:24). He doesn't live in a physical body like ours, so He is not impressed with the way our physical bodies look. He does want us to take good care of our bodies. Our bodies house His Spirit (Rom. 8:11). We must take good care of our bodies so that we will live long on the earth (Ps. 91:16). Still, I have been pleasantly surprised to find out God does not hold beauty contests. He holds heart contests. The contest or the challenge is not whether my heart can beat out your heart or your heart can beat out my heart. It is not a competition between you and your parents or you and your children.

The contest is not against people. God is the Judge and the only thing He is going to judge in my life is me. The only thing He is going to judge in your life is you. Can you keep your heart pure in His sight? It is a challenge.

<u>Revenge Is an Enemy of Love</u>

As I have said before, revenge creates an impure heart. According to Webster's Dictionary, revenge is to inflict damage, injury, or punishment in return for an injury, insult, etc. The idea of getting back at someone is at the heart of revenge. We think we are the ones getting even, but revenge is a very subtle tool the devil uses against God's people.

God says that revenge belongs to Him and that He would repay the person or people who have done us wrong (Rom. 12:19; Heb. 10:30). Revenge in your heart prevents you from being rightly motivated in your relationships. Revenge in your heart prevents you from being rightly related to God, and if you are not rightly related to God you are under the curse.

Maybe you feel powerless. It seems the curse is in control of your life. Trace your steps. James 4:7 says submit (or surrender) yourself now unto God and resist the devil and he will flee. Are you submitting to God? Are you resisting the devil? Most people don't want the curse or bad things to come against their lives. However, most people are not aware that unresolved anger, or unforgiveness, opens the door to the devil and the curse to come into their lives. Because they are not resisting strife, they are not resisting the devil and the curse.

They are actually resisting God. You cannot get God's blessing without God's way of thinking. You cannot get God's blessings when you try to be God. In Isaiah 45:22 (NLT) God says, "Let all the world look to me for salvation! For I am God; there is no other." Most of us are not foolish enough to say that we are God, but many times our behavior speaks louder than our words. The issue is a matter of the heart.

Go to prayer meetings. Read The Bible. Those are good "things" to do. But are you doing them out of a pure heart? I don't want to do just what I want to do. I want to do what God wants me to do and I want to do it the way He wants me to do it. Moses cried, "Lord, teach me Your ways" (Ex. 33:13). Are you living your life in sensitivity to what the Spirit of God is telling you? God is always showing us His ways. The Bible is His personal plan to show each one of us what He wants from us (Jos. 1:8).

Many times we want to impress God with our "works." We have good works to do (II Thess. 2:17) and our good works show that we have faith in God (Jas. 2:14-26). Still, good works do not impress God. God is impressed when we "do justly, love mercy and walk humbly with Him" (Micah 6:8). Our ability to maintain relationships is what impresses God (I Jn. 4:21).

It awes me to know how simple God is. God is simple. He made mighty mountains. He made the sea. He set the laws of gravity in place. Yet He is so concerned about how we treat one another. In John 15:12 Jesus said, "This is My commandment that you love one another." If love is not your foundation, you are on sinking sand. God is love (I Jn. 4:8, 16). God's love is a pure love flowing from a pure heart.

Revenge comes from an impure heart; however, it is a trait common to fallen man. We come into this world looking out for Number One. If our parents were revengeful people, then we probably are revengeful people. If your parents didn't correct you when they saw you act in a revengeful way, you probably grew to be a revengeful person.

Revenge taints love. You can love someone, honestly love someone, but if you have a revengeful heart, you will not be able to love that person purely. Purity is an issue many associate with virginity of the body, but purity is also an issue of the heart.

When we have "one heart" with family members we are very supportive of them. Revenge hinders support for one another. The Lord asked me one time how "for" my husband could I be. To be "for" someone means to support that person. Wives are called to be cheerleaders. I said I loved him. I said in my vows that in sickness and in health, richer and poorer, in good times and bad times I would be for him. But when I was angry with him I was not for him. When I was angry I was not acting in a loving way toward him. When I was angry the impurities in my heart rose to the top. It is said that when gold is fired up the impurities rise to the top. Well, God doesn't want our impurities to rise to the top. He wants our purity to rise to the top. He wants our love to rise to the top.

I first really understood that my love was not rising to the top when I was angry with my husband. The impurities were there before I got married, but it was after I got married that I began to recognize them as impurities. So many times we discount our bad attitudes with our parents or our siblings. We discount the bad attitudes because we didn't choose those people. We need to realize that how we treat those people is only practice for life apart from those people.

So even though I could be disrespectful at home, I didn't understand that I was really wrong for having that attitude. I knew I was wrong, but I didn't feel really wrong. I realized I was really wrong for that attitude after I displayed it against the man I had chosen.

Otha is the man that I have chosen to live with for the rest of my life. The Lord showed me that many times when I was angry with him that I disrespected him. I wouldn't talk to him nicely or I wouldn't talk to him at all. Many times even though I felt that my husband was wrong, I have had to repent to my husband and God for my disrespectful attitude.

When we disrespect our family members we stop valuing our family members. We stop loving them. The issue of who's right and who's wrong needs to be forgotten if the love toward your spouse, children or parents is going to stop. When we stop loving our family members we hurt them emotionally. I don't want to hurt my family. Now I am quick to resolve issues and quick to forgive offenses. I tell my husband, my children, myself, God and the devil that I am the most forgiving person. I do this to keep my heart pure.

Pure Love Does Not Want to Cause Any More Pain

A pure heart produces pure love. Pure love does not want to cause pain. The prayer of Jabez was that he not be the cause of any more pain (I Chr. 4:9, 10). Jabez's mother remembered the pain of his childbirth. Unless a mother has had a Cesarean section, most mothers do not remember the pain of childbirth. Jabez's mother remembered the pain of his childbirth and even caused him to know about it. Jabez prayed that he would not cause pain. I believe because Jabez was sensitive to pain, he was sensitive to love. Love does not want to hurt others. Jabez did not want to cause pain. The Bible says God did for Jabez what he asked. Have you prayed not to cause others pain?

We need to consistently examine our hearts to maintain its purity. Many of us have not experienced pure love, but lust. Lust is a spirit of control. By control, I mean a person may have a legitimate need, but then try to get the need satisfied by illegitimate or ungodly means. For example, you may really need your child's cooperation, but instead of asking for cooperation, you angrily demand his help, thus hurting his feelings. Or say you want your parents to love you, but you sleep around trying to be loved, thus distancing yourself from your parents. Your actions display that your true motivation was not to give love, but to take love from someone else. You are trying to control others' actions toward you.

In the God-kind of love, a person's motivation will be to give love. In a godly marriage, the husband and the wife's motivation will be to give love to their mates. In godly households, the parents' motivation will be to give love to their children. In any godly relationship, the people involved will be motivated to give pure love. Pure love goes beyond feelings. Pure love goes beyond just seeing what I can get out of the other person. Pure love is rooted in the emotional support I can give to another person.

In order to consistently give that kind of love, one must consistently receive the love of God. You receive the love of God by spending a lot of time with Him. You may say, "I have been a Christian a long time. I have received the love of God, but yet the curse of poverty still holds onto me." You say, "I have received the love of God, but my children are still not saved." You say, "I have received the love of God, but I still get angry easily."

You need a greater revelation of the love of God to flow through your life. Faith works by love (Gal. 5:6). There are promises in the Bible for every area of our lives such as prosperity (Deut. 8:18), children (Isa.54:13), and peace (Jn. 14:27). We tap into those promises with our love.

How is our love walk when we don't have the money we need? How do we treat our children when they say they don't want to go to church? Are we pouring out God's love then? Or are we pouring out revenge against them because they are not doing what we want?

God Wants Us to Love Others

You can mentally assent to the fact that God loves you, but the proof will be in how you act toward other people. Your heart will show the proof of what you believe. The belief most people have of loving someone is the belief of convenience. If it is convenient for me to love then I will. A lot of women want princes who will take care of them financially and socially. But what happens when they find out that prince charming is sloppy? Where is the love? A lot of men want a beautiful woman that they can make love to all day long. But what happens when her career puts her marriage on the back burner? Where is the love when it is not convenient to love?

The lack of loving responses is the cause for hurt feelings or feeling rejected. To prevent themselves from being rejected many people have shorted themselves on long-lasting, meaningful relationships. They are skittish towards the idea of committed love. In order to sustain our relationships we have to draw on the love of God. He is very committed to us. He is not going to hurt us. He does not love for the sake of convenience. For God so loved the world that He gave His only begotten Son (Jn. 3:16). Does that sound like convenience to you? No, to me it sounds like Someone who is truly "for" you. The Bible says if God is for us—and I have good news, God is for us—then who can be against us? (Rom. 8:31).

The answer is no one. No one can hurt us when we have received the love of God. I don't mean that our feelings will never be hurt again. But I mean we will be more concerned that we don't hurt other people's feelings than we will be if they hurt our feelings. God says that since Jesus laid down His life for us, we should lay down our lives for our brothers, our sisters, our mothers, our fathers and our children (I Jn. 3:16).

God commands that we love one another (Jn. 15:12). When Jesus hung on the cross He wasn't having a vacation. He was being obedient to God's Word so that you and I could experience the ever-lasting love of God (Jer. 31:3). He was being obedient to God's

Word so that you and I could give the kind of love that doesn't stop. First Corinthians 13:4-7 in the Living Bible says:

> Love is very patient, love is kind. It is never jealous or envious. It is not boastful or proud.
>
> It is not haughty, selfish or rude. Love does not demand its own way. It is not irritable or touchy. It does not hold grudges and will hardly even notice when others do it wrong.
>
> It is never glad about injustice, but rejoices when truth wins out.
>
> If you love someone (*your son, daughter, husband, mother and father*), you will be loyal to him (*them*) no matter what the cost. You will always believe in him (*them*). You will always expect the best of him (*them*). You will always stand your ground in defending him (*them*).

Purely loving someone is not easy. Pure love like pure gold only comes out with work, with effort. It is not hard to be patient with my child who is doing everything "right." It is when she is trying my patience that I need to enforce my love for her. When she is doing what I want her to do I want to be patient. I want to be loving. But when she is not doing what I want her to do and doing the opposite of what I want her to do, my love is exposed. My heart is exposed. Are my motives pure?

Impure motives of undermining my parents' authority or belittling my children every time they do something I think is offensive are not motivated by love. The love has stopped. It is natural for the love to stop. Humans can not in their own strength love all of the time, but we can love for a very long time when we have the supernatural love of God. We can continue to love our parents in spite of their behavior if we draw on God's love. We can continue to love our mates in spite of their behavior if we draw on God's love. We can continue to love our children in spite of their behavior if we draw on God's love. In fact, we need to draw on God's love to live in this world.

We Can Resist Love

God loves people. He wants us to love people. Many times, however, when we are angry not only do we resist giving love, but we also resist receiving love. We have all seen a child resist being hugged after he has been told "no." That child is resisting love. That child is angry. The Bible says, "Be angry, but do not sin" (Eph. 4:26). We could interpret that to also mean "Be angry, but do not stop loving. Be angry, but do not become impatient. Be angry, but do not be unkind."

When we resist receiving love we are being unkind. When we resist receiving love we are in sin. God commands us to love and when we stop receiving love, we stop giving love. We are no longer behaving in a loving manner. We are rejecting love.

We reject our family members more than anyone else. We take revenge against our family members more than anyone else. We get angry with our family members more than anyone else.

The Bible doesn't say that Eve was angry with God when she ate the apple, but we do know that when the devil tempted Eve He was tempting her out of revenge against God. He told her that God was holding back something from her and she believed him (Gen. 3:1-6). When Adam and Eve sinned against God, they did it with the devil's motivation. At the heart of rejection is revenge.

In Luke Chapter 9, the account was given of a time when Jesus and His disciples were heading for Jerusalem, but they were planning to stop at this certain Samaritan village. The people of that village did not receive them and the rejection from those people angered the disciples who then wanted to destroy the village by calling down fire from heaven. They wanted revenge. In verses 55-56, "But He (Jesus) turned, and rebuked them, and said, 'You know not what manner of spirit you are of. For the Son of man is not come to destroy men's lives, but to save them.' And they went to another village."

In John 21:15-17, Jesus asked Peter three times, "Do you love Me?" Three times. The same question. Why did Jesus ask Peter so many times the same question? Let's put it into context. Only a few days earlier Peter had watched helplessly as Jesus was crucified by the people. He didn't feel love for those people. He had gone back to fishing.

"Peter, do you love Me?" Why was that such a difficult question?

Because Peter, like many others, believed that you can love God without loving people. Earlier Jesus had told Peter that he would fish for men. Yet there he was fishing for fish. After Peter affirmed that he did love Him, Jesus told him to feed His people. He told him to love the people.

You cannot separate loving God from loving people. When we love God we will love other people. Paul prayed that we might know the height, depth, length, and breadth of God's love (Eph. 3:17-19).

God Loves You

To most people the concept of love is good. Most people are looking for love. But when God gives His love He also gives His ways (Jn. 14:15). He cares how we treat each other. Again, He is not impressed with our works. He is impressed with our love.

God's ways are pure. He is the original Mr. Goody Two Shoes. First John 1:5 says, "God is light and in Him there is no darkness at all." That means that He only wants to help you walk in His ways. He wants you to be in the light as He is in the light (I Jn. 1:7).

Being in the light means that we will have no hidden motives. Being in the light means that we will purely love one another (I Pet. 1:22). Examine the relationships you have with your parents, with your spouse and your children. Are they pure? Are they tainted with revenge?

Draw on the love of God so that you can give it away. When you draw on the love of God you draw on God himself. He is strong. He can be depended on. He loves you.

Here is how to biblically walk in love with others:

1. Tell them you love them. The Bible says that out of the abundance of your heart your mouth will speak (Matt. 12:34). The words "I love you" mean so much to your family members.

2. Acknowledge that people are different. The way I think may not be the same way you think, but I can still love and appreciate you even if I don't agree with you. When you disagree, strive to be resolution-minded. The ability to stay calm will help you convey love to your parent, spouse or child.

3. Realize your eyes are the window to your soul. How you feel is often expressed through your eyes. If you are trying to convey love, look lovingly at the person you are talking to. "Jesus, beholding him, loved him" (Mark 10:21).

4. Seek out what makes that person feel loved. Gary Chapman has written an excellent book *The Five Love Languages* to help people discern how they receive love. The five love languages are: words of affirmation, touch, quality time, acts of service, and gifts.

    a. "Words of Affirmation" are kind words. Words that make the person feel good. To your spouse: "Honey, you make the best pancakes." To a child: "You are an artist." They are sincere words said to make the person feel good.

    b. "Touch" is touching a person in a gentle way. Touching in non-sexual and sexual ways. My husband likes to touch my face. He likes to pick up and carry our children.

    c. "Quality Time" is spending specific time with a person. This is my love language and my mother makes me feel so loved when she takes the time to visit me. I am giving my love when I sit and read with my children.

    d. "Acts of Service" is a giving of self. A person who likes acts of service really appreciates his wife ironing his shirt. A wife really appreciates the husband vacuuming. This love wants help and wants to help.

    e. "Gifts" is receiving things from and giving things to others. The person who receives love this way likes small gifts and big gifts. They like to give and receive gifts. The man who gives his wife flowers. The little boy whose dad gives him an interesting rock. This love likes "new" things.

Please keep in mind that though some people speak one of the love languages more than others, all of the love languages are needed to make a person feel truly loved.

God's Word on Walking in Love:

I have loved you with an everlasting love. (Jer. 33:3)

For God so loved the world that He sent His only begotten son that whosoever believeth on Him shall live and not perish. (Jn. 3:16 KJV)

God is love. (I Jn. 4:8)

If you love God, you will obey Him. (Jn. 14:15)

Love your neighbor as you love yourself. (Lev. 19:18)

Nourishing Your Family

The Bible talks about two kinds of nourishment that God provides for His children. One is natural nourishment. God made food for us to eat. Exodus 16:15 says that God gave the children of Israel manna to eat after they left Egypt. The second form of nourishment is your career or calling. God has a specific job that He has assigned each one of us to do. Jesus said, "My food is to do the will of God" (Jn. 4:34). God is clearly concerned that we eat food and He is clearly concerned that we do His will.

Natural Food Is Comforting

Natural food has an important function in everyone's life. Food fills the stomach, which in turn feeds the body. The comfort of the body feeds the emotions, which in turn feeds the soul. We all have heard of comfort foods. These are foods you eat just because you like to eat them. They may or may not have any nutritional value. You just like them. They fill your stomach and they fill your emotional need for comfort.

God gives us food to show that He cares for us (Gen. 2:9). His commitment to care for our deepest, most natural sense of comfort shows He cares for us. The same commitment can occur when we have events that include food. Pastors transmit commitment when they allow church dinners. Heads of families transmit commitment when they organize a family reunion. Food is a unifying agent in the earth. Eating is perhaps the one thing almost everyone likes to do.

Although I like home cooking, I like to eat at restaurants. I like to eat without any concern of preparation or cleanup. I do have to concern myself with the bill, but sometimes I am willing to trade money for food served with a smile. Having a good meal served to me is so satisfying to my soul. It brings me comfort.

Children often not only want comfort, but they also only want comfort foods. Yet children need to eat a variety of foods and not just comfort foods. As we see obesity running high among children, we must be cautious to train our families to eat to live and not live to eat. When we feed our children we must remember that we are not just feeding their bodies, but also feeding their souls. When we feed our children we are serving them.

How you present food to your children is very important. Think of a restaurant. If the waitress sloshes your food down in front of you, how would you feel? When we serve our children remember they receive this act of service as an expression of love. Don't send mixed messages to your children when you serve them breakfast, lunch, dinner or even snacks.

God Has Made Food in Great Supply

When children are physically undernourished they blame their parents. Children do not understand poverty. They do not understand why their needs are not getting met, especially if the parents are telling them they love them. They get confused when words and deeds do not add up. When children are confused the curse has access into their lives. A person with a greedy spirit almost always experienced a lack of food in childhood.

Food is not in short supply for God. In Matthew 16:6-12 we read the account of when Jesus scolded the disciples for thinking that He was concerned about food.

> Then Jesus said unto them, Take heed and beware of the leaven of the Pharisees and of the Sadducees.
>
> And they reasoned among themselves, saying, It is because we have taken no bread.
>
> Which when Jesus perceived, he said unto them, O ye of little faith, why reason ye among yourselves, because ye have brought no bread?
>
> Do ye not yet understand, neither remember the five loaves of the five thousand, and how many baskets ye took up?
>
> Neither the seven loaves of the four thousand, and how many baskets ye took up?
>
> How is it that ye do not understand that I spake it not to you concerning bread, that ye should beware of the leaven of the Pharisees and of the Sadducees?

Then understood they how that he bade them not beware of the leaven of bread, but of the doctrine of the Pharisees and of the Sadducees. (KJV)

There are people starving all over the world and there are even children of God who barely get by nutritionally. This should not be. Psalms 37:25 says, "I have never seen the righteous forsaken nor his seed begging bread." Natural circumstances are almost always a condition of spiritual circumstances. When we don't live our lives the way God would have us to live our lives we often don't receive His provision that He has prepared for our lives.

God has already provided for our basic needs. Food is plentiful in the earth. Food is such a basic necessity to life that overindulgence can turn what is meant to be a blessing into curse. Many illnesses are the result of improper diet. Eating too much food can lead to illness. Eating too much food can even lead to obesity. Not only physically do obese people have more problems with their bodies than people who eat in moderation, many obese people are rejected because of the size of their bodies. Rejection is in indicator that the curse of disunity is operating in a person's life. This is not condemnation for you if you are overweight. I am simply pointing out that when we are being overindulgent in food can cause the curse of disunity to operate our lives.

You Can Live Without Food

People can be literally overindulgent or they can be spiritually overindulgent concerning food. When people are literally overindulgent they eat too much. When people are spiritually overindulgent concerning food, they will not fast. They will not deny themselves food. They must eat. They feel they might die if they don't eat.

When you fast your body may act like its dying, yet your body will not die. Your dependence on food will decrease and your dependence on God will increase. God wants us to put Him first in every area of our lives (Matt. 6:33).

Fasting puts a great demand on God to take care of you. I don't mean that you are demanding anything from God. Rather, when you are fasting you are putting a demand on the promises that God has made. You are putting a greater dependence on God to take care of you. He said I would never leave you nor forsake you (Heb. 13:5). When you fast God will prove that He will take care of you (I Pet. 5:7).

Fasting is a refraining from food or any thing that you like a lot. You could fast TV if you watch it a lot. You could fast sweets if you eat them a lot. Fasting is simply a way to say to God, "I depend on You for the pleasure, comfort or help I would otherwise get from this thing." I am not advocating long periods of time without eating. God made our bodies to need food. Our bodies can become ill when we take long periods of time not eating.

In the beginning of Jesus' earthly ministry He fasted for 40 days. That is a long time. He didn't become ill, but the Bible does say that after 40 days strange things manifested. The Bible says the devil came to him (Matt. 4:3-11). When we fast the purpose is not for the devil to come to us, but for God to come to us in a fresh way. When we are fasting we are not only refraining from food, but we are also praying unto God. (I discuss prayer in a greater detail in the last chapter.) When we fast we want to hear from God more clearly.

Now we don't condemn Jesus for fasting a long time. He was preparing to save the world. He needed to hear from God and I believe if He had fasted five days the devil would have come to Him. As the Savior of the world, He had to face the devil. When we fast we want to face anything in our lives that is not like God. We want to face confusion, selfish ambition, unrighteous anger and any other vice that hinders us from living in unity with our family members.

When we fast in order to have family unity, God knows that we are serious. He knows that we really do want family unity. We can fast for specific direction from God and we can have a lifestyle of fasting. To have a lifestyle of fasting a person would skip one meal a day once a week and pray during the time you would have eaten. (If you have diabetes, are pregnant or have some other health issue that you cannot fast a meal, seek the Lord about what type of food you can fast.) A lifestyle of fasting helps you function better in life. It helps you to better understand God's will for your life.

God Has a Plan

Doing God's will is spiritual food. Jesus said, "My food is to do the Father's will" (Jn. 4:34). Do you know what God's will is for your life? Are you doing it? In order to walk in the blessings of Abraham we must have Abraham's kind of obedience. In order to walk in the blessings of Abraham, we must do the will of God (Matt. 7:21).

God has a plan for every person. (Jer. 29:11) He has given every person natural talents. A talented person with effort can accomplish great things. Some people are even gifted. A gifted person without much effort can accomplish great things. But not everyone recognizes their talents and gifts are from God and therefore, they are not doing His will with them.

In order to be successful in life, we must do God's will (I Jn. 2:17). When we have done one thing that He said to do, then He will show us the next thing He wants us to do. Many people get nervous when someone mentions "God's will." They say, "You never know what God is going to do. God is so big and powerful He can do whatever He wants." That is true. God is big and powerful. What is not true is that He can do whatever He wants. If He could, He would perform His will whenever He wanted. Philippians 2:13 says God works in us to will and to do His good pleasure. He waits for us to want His will and He waits on us to do His will.

The average American does not tolerate someone else dictating his life. This is a democracy. Let the will of the people be done. In his 2005 inaugural speech, President George W. Bush talked about America's fight for freedom. I heard a commentator respond after the speech that freedom does not mean the same thing to everyone, so to say America was fighting for freedom was too broad a statement.

Freedom can mean a wide spectrum of things to different people. However, for a Christian, freedom is to be free to do what God wants you to do (Gal. 5:1). The problem with freedom is that people think they are free to do whatever they want to do. They are not even listening to hear if God is telling them to do something. Did you know God speaks? (Ex. 6:29). Not out loud usually, but in your heart, through your thoughts. God will tell you what you need to know when you need to know it. He speaks to His children. He speaks to those who obey Him (Ps. 85:8).

What has God been saying to you lately about your job? Is He saying stay? Is He saying go? Is He saying get more training? Is He calling you into the ministry?

God is Sovereign (Ps. 97:1). He is Almighty (Gen. 17:1). He is the creator of heaven and earth (Gen. 1:1). He knows what we should be doing and when. When we do His vision for our lives we will live richer, fuller lives than we ever could possibly live without doing His vision.

Many times we ask little children what they want to be when they grow up. Some say, "I want to be a doctor, or a firefighter or a ballerina." But most do not say, "I need to ask God." We program our children to believe that they can be whatever they want to be and to an extent this is true. They have talents. They have gifts. Still, the gifts and callings are from God; therefore we should train our children at an early age to ask God what He wants them to do with His gifts (Rom. 11:29). Everything we have God gave us. We are not owners of anything, merely stewards. I am not the owner of my writing skills. I am only a steward. I can only write what God tells me to write.

What is your calling? What are your skills, talents, gifts? Are you using them to bring honor to God who gave them to you? Or are you using them only to make money? Or are you using them only to please people? Again this goes back to your motivation. Jesus said, "My food is to do the will of My Father." Many people mistake their jobs to be their will. Some mistake their jobs to be drudgery. Jesus gives us the motivation for why we work in Matthew 25:14-30:

To the one he gave five talents of money, to another two talents, and to another one talent, each according to his ability. Then he went on his journey. The man who had received the five talents went at once and put his money to work and gained five more. So also the one with the two talents gained two more. But the man who had received the one talent went off, dug a hole in the ground and hid his master's money.

After a long time the master of those servants returned and settled accounts with them. The man who had received the five talents brought the other five. "Master," he said, "you **entrusted** me with five talents. See, I have gained five more."

His master replied, "Well done, good and faithful servant! You have been faithful with a few things; I will put you in charge of many things. Come and share your master's happiness!"

The man with the two talents also came. "Master," he said, "you **entrusted** me with two talents; see, I have gained two more."

His master replied, "Well done, good and faithful servant! You have been faithful with a few things; I will put you in charge of many things. Come and share your master's happiness!"

The man who had received the one talent came. "Master," he said, "I knew that you are a hard man, harvesting where you have not sown and gathering where you have not scattered seed. So I was afraid and went out and hid your talent in the ground. See, here is what belongs to you."

His master replied, "You wicked, lazy servant! So you knew that I harvest where I have not sown and gather where I have not scattered seed? Well then, you should have put my money on deposit with the bankers so that when I returned I would have received it back with interest.

"Take the talent from him and give it to the one who has the ten talents. For everyone who has will be given more and he will have an abundance. Whoever does not have, even what he has will be taken from him. And throw that worthless servant outside, into the darkness, where there will be weeping and gnashing of teeth."

God has entrusted us with specific gifts and talents. He expects everyone's work to be for Him (Eph. 6:6). Just as people who eat more than they need can become overweight, people who have talents that they don't use for God can become bitter. Some people are so ungrateful for their jobs. They make all kinds of excuses for not going to work. These people have unhealthy souls.

<u>Laziness Is Not an Option</u>

Proverbs 26:13 says the slothful says there is a lion in the street. There is not a lion in the street. The slothful simply do not want to go out. The slothful simply do not want to work (Prov. 21:25). Everything about work is not going to be pleasant, but when your reason for working is to bring glory to God, the work in general will be pleasant. Everything about your profession will not be pleasant, but the people will be pleasant. The atmosphere where you work will be pleasant.

When your reason for working is to bring glory to God, grace will be on you so that you don't complain about the problems on your job. Grace is God's power flowing through your life to overcome the problems. Grace will be on you so that you pray about the problems at work. Grace will be on you to pray for your co-workers and your bosses. Complaining is immature. Again, immaturity means to be underdeveloped in the area of maintaining good relationships. If you complain a lot about your job, you show that your parents did not nurture you. You show they did not teach you how to stand for good relationships.

Everything you learned about relationships you learned from your parents. Having a good job is based on having good relationships with the people around you. If you have a good relationship with your parents, you will have a good relationship with the people on your job. If poverty is part of your childhood, your parents did not teach you a good working relationship with other people. You may or may not be poor right now; still, if poverty is part of your background your parents did not teach you unity. Psalms 133:1-3 says, "How good and pleasant it is when the brethren dwell in unity..." There God commands the blessing – the empowerment to prosper.

Second Thessalonians 3:10 says if you don't work you don't eat. In order to eat you must work. Poverty in America is the result of people not working. This is the most blessed nation in the world. If you can make it anywhere, it is here in America. Many people come from other countries to get jobs here. There are plenty of jobs in America.

This is not a message of condemnation. There are reasons why people do not work at a job. But there are no excuses of why people don't work at something. There are different kinds of work. I work at home with my children and sometimes at a part-time daycare with other people's children. My husband works for a corporation. We both are working. I am not getting paid very much for my work. My husband is getting paid a lot for his work. I work so I eat. He works so he eats. The principle of work is not about wages. Different people will make different wages. The principle of work is using your gifts and talents to honor God.

Excel in Your Work

When my brother hurt his back on his job, he decided to finish his college degree. He couldn't work in the field where he had been working; therefore he worked on his degree. His wife worked a regular job. They both worked. They both ate. Again, the issue is not about the pay of the work. Some jobs don't pay very much. Most fast food restaurants do not pay a lot, but you get to eat for free when you work in those establishments. Fast food restaurants offer promotions at a fast rate also. If you excel in your work, you will be promoted.

You may say, "But my gift, my talent is not to work in a fast food establishment. I am trained for this or that." The truth of it is you may be trained in an area, but if you cannot find a job in that area you may be trained in the wrong profession. Or you may need to humble yourself (I Pet. 5:6). Joseph was a man God planned to rule over his brothers (Gen. 37:5). Yet before he did that he was sold as a slave, slandered, and sent to prison (Gen. 37:23-39:20).

It always amazes me to think of Paul the apostle writing letters from prison to help others. Many of us think people in prison need help. Paul's life mission was to help people so even in prison he continued to help people (Eph. 3:1). Lazy people have no desire to work (Prov. 21:25). Laziness leads to poverty. Poverty is a condition of the mind. Proverbs 23:7 says as a man thinks in his heart so is he. If self-pity is your consistent mode of thinking, you will be poor. A poverty mentality creates poverty in your life. A "poor me" mentality creates poverty in your life.

Joseph could have said, "Poor me. I have been falsely accused." Yet when the butler and baker got thrown into the prison, there he was using his talent of administration (Gen. 40:1-3). Joseph was basically running the prison (Gen. 39:21-23). He wasn't feeling sorry for himself because he wasn't where he wanted to be. You can use your talent or gift anywhere, and when you excel in it you will rise. After Joseph was able to interpret Pharaoh's dream, he was promoted to prime minister. Pharaoh did not concern himself with Egypt. Egypt was in Joseph's hands (Gen. 41:38-44).

Although Joseph had a spiritual gift of interpreting dreams, his natural talent was in administration. Many people want to live on the spiritual gift when the spiritual gift will only help excel you in your natural talent. We are spiritually gifted to help people using our natural talents.

As I have said before, God relates to us both spiritually and naturally. When we acknowledge Him spiritually He will acknowledge us naturally. He said those who honor Me (spiritually) I will honor him (naturally) (I Sam. 2:30). He said if you see a man who is diligent in his skill, he will stand before kings. He will not stand before mere men (Prov. 22:29).

The Lord Will Guide You in Your Employment

It is a blessing to know what God's will is for one's life. Parents who do the will of God pass a blessing to their children. Maybe your parents did not know God had a plan for their lives. Maybe your parents never told you that God had a plan for your life. Maybe you were not aware that God wanted to use your life. Right now I am writing to tell you that doing God's will is what you were created for.

Many people do not know to ask God what it is He wants them to do. They simply say, "I am good at this so this is what I am going to do." James 4:3-4 says you have not because you ask not or you ask with the wrong motive. There are many people unfulfilled in their professions because they keep banging their heads against a wall in the wrong profession. Some people believe they can kick down the door to their professional happiness. Unfortunately, the wall in the wrong profession has no door.

Revelation 3:8 says that the Lord opens doors that no man can shut. When God has something for you to do, there is nothing that can stop you from doing it except you. When the Israelites crossed the Jordan to face Jericho they were no match for Jericho. Jericho was a walled city. However, God gave them a strategy and the walls fell down in front of them (Jos. 6:5). They didn't kick at the wall. They didn't stand and cry in front of the wall. They marched. They yelled. They simply did what God told them to do and God did the rest.

The wrong profession is primarily the result of not asking the Lord to show you your talents and the profession that you can impact the most with them. If you are a good talker, there are a myriad of professions you could do talking. There are talkers in every profession, but if you are a talker stuck in one room with a computer all day you may not be the happiest employee of the company. You may not be reaching your fullest potential.

Parents can help or hinder their children in reaching their fullest potential. A parent with good self-esteem will encourage her daughter to pursue her dreams. A parent with poor self-esteem could hold her daughter back from pursuing her dreams. A parent with good self-esteem will encourage his son to challenge his skills. A parent with poor self-esteem could also push his son into the wrong profession. Parents should ask God to show them the plan He has for their children and should encourage their children to follow God's plan.

When a child is born out of wedlock many times that child will wander in life. The lack of the holy "yes" can keep them from believing that God, the God of the universe, could actually have a good plan for them. Single parents especially, remember that rejection is not just natural; it is also spiritual. Although children being raised in a two-parent family will experience rejection, single-parented children have a greater difficulty with rejection.

In general, rejection can cause you not to believe in yourself or it can cause you to "over-believe" in yourself. You could also reject your job or be unfulfilled in it if you asked amiss for it. God wants you to be rightly motivated in everything you do - your profession included. If you chose your profession based on money, you were wrongly motivated. Money should not be our motive for doing anything. Remember, Luke 12:15 says, "Beware all kinds of greed."

Again, I'm not saying if you are an expert in a field, you should take the lowest position available in that field because you do not want the money. You want the best that God can give you, including the best pay. Work, however, is not just about pay. Work is about helping others (I Thess. 4:11-12). And if having a high position will cause you to become big headed, perhaps you should take a lower position. God can help us reach a high level (Matt. 6:3). In fact, part of the blessing is to be the head and not the tail. Yet God does not want us to be conceited, haughty or arrogant because of our pay or high position (I Pet. 5:5).

God wants our motives for everything we do to be pure (Phil. 2:3). If your motive in your profession is not to meet a need by helping people, you should repent. It could be that you are in the right profession. You can do the tasks with ease. You may have even been rewarded for your performance. Still, God has called all His children to have the same heart about working. He wants the preacher, the teacher, the plumber, the convenience store clerk, and all fields of workers to work to help people for His glory. When a person excels in meeting needs, his pay will increase.

Again, God will bless us in whatever profession we are in as long as it brings Him glory. Before I became a student at Oral Roberts University, I believed the "hand of the Lord" could only be on preachers. I was happy to see that the university provided training for a variety of professions with the mission for the students to go into every man's world.

Be Thankful For Your Job

At ORU I began to see how the spiritual life and the natural life were supposed to connect. Most people want either a spiritual life or a natural life, but the two cannot be separated. Some people are so spiritually-minded that they are no earthly good, and some people are so earthly-minded that they are not spiritually good. God created us to be spirit, body and soul. We are natural people with a spiritual connection to God.

God wants you to be thankful for your profession (Ecc. 2:24). He wants you to make a difference to the people around you. He wants you to love, to nourish, and to nurture those in your profession. A person in a profession just for the money will not be thankful. That type of person will be too consumed with himself. That type of person will be selfish, angry and confused in trying to achieve success in his profession. The profession that God plans for you will be a place where you are in unity with the people around you.

The people in your life should be able to see your abilities, starting with your parents. Parents should be able to see their children's abilities. This is not to say that parents should tell their children what their profession is. However, they can and should nourish (encourage) their children's abilities.

Early in life ability in talents and gifts emerge. At my son's school starting in kindergarten, they give out character awards. The teachers are trained to look for the children's talents to emerge at a young age. I have asked God to show me which activities to let my children be involved in. I don't want them to float in life when God has a specific plan for them that He is willing to tell my husband and me and them about.

You Can Live a Fulfilled Life

I floated in life a little while. I transferred to ORU in the early 90's from a state university. I knew I liked to write. I thought I also liked television production. I thought I wanted to be a television reporter. When I got to ORU, I realized that I did not want to be a television reporter. To be a television reporter you have to really like to talk. I have never been a big talker. Still, by earning a Communication Arts degree, I learned that there are different types of talking. There are different ways of communicating. I am a big talker through the written word.

As I realized that I liked to write then I had to get specific with what kind of writing that I wanted to write. I didn't want to write the news, although I could. I didn't want to write fiction, although I could. I mainly wanted to write non-fiction. I mainly wanted to write things that helped people to grow in their walk with God. I married in June towards the end of my senior year and it wasn't long afterwards that God birthed the idea in me of writing for families. Writing to help families is what I like to do.

Maybe you are unfulfilled because you have not been specific in what you like to do. If I had written fiction, I would not have been fulfilled. If I had written the news, I would not have been fulfilled. I needed to write nonfiction for spiritual growth to be fulfilled.

God's good plan for your life is that you be fulfilled (Ps. 145:19). Don't settle for an unsatisfying job. However, don't let unsatisfying prospects prevent you from working. If you can't find the job of your dreams, take what you can find and refine your talents and gifts. God will promote those who excel in their work. God will open doors where you can use your talents and gifts to the fullest.

If God is leading you to make a change in your profession or even change your profession, fear not (Gen. 15:1)! He will provide everything you need (Phil. 4:19). All you have to do is supply the heart to do His will (Eph. 6:6). He who began a good work in you is faithful to complete it (Phil. 1:6).

Your life is not over until it is over. You may have lived many places. You may have had many jobs. Yet the purposes of God for your life will come to pass (Isa. 25:1). Even if you chose the wrong profession or chose a profession for the wrong reason, it is not too late to make your life count for eternity. It is not too late for you to live your life to help others.

Here are a few godly ways to nourish your family members:

1. Feed your family members nourishing foods. Food is a high priority to most people. Giving others food is greatly appreciated. Have times when you eat with others. Don't make it a habit to eat only with your family. Invite people to lunch. Invite people to your house for dinner. Sharing a meal is a great way to express your love to others.
2. Attend a family reunion. Family reunions are of God. They are ordained to bring the whole family together. They are

ordained to keep the family unified. They are ordained to provide a place where the whole family can share in the bountifulness of God. The food is usually very good, too!

3. Nourish the vision of your family members. Some people are just floating in life, but as you see their gifts and their talents, encourage those people to use those gifts and talents for the Lord. The happiest people are those who are using their gifts and talents for the Lord.

4. Study the motive gifts so that you recognize them in your family members. The Bible tells us there are seven ways people are motivated to help other people. They are listed in Romans 12:6-8:

    a. Prophecy – these people help others discern right from wrong. They hate compromise. They see things as black or white. These people help others understand right from wrong.

    b. Teaching – these people train others. They help others understand how to do the right thing.

    c. Exhorting – these people encourage others. They will help keep people motivated to do the right thing.

    d. Giving – these people make a lot of money. They help people fund projects.

    e. Administrating – these people organize people. They can help fit people in the right positions.

    f. Serving – these people help others with their practical needs. They are the first to offer help.

    g. Mercy – these people want to soothe others. They want others to know how much they are cared for.

It has been said that the motive gifts are gifts that represent different aspects of God. God is all of these things. He is merciful. He encourages us. He puts up one and sets down another (Ps. 75:7). Everything we have and we are come from God.

In the area you are motivationally gifted, you will also be spiritually discerning. You will have revelation in that area. Revelation is knowledge given to you directly by God in conjunction with your gift. Joseph's ability to interpret dreams was revelation knowledge from God to make him wise as he helped others using his gift of administration.

God will give you revelation concerning your job when you keep the desire to help others as your motivation. And remember: how well you eat is directly related to how well you work.

God's Word on Food and Vision:

> God gives seed to the sower and bread to the eater. (Isa. 55:10 KJV)

> Let your light so shine before men, that they may see your good works, and glorify your Father which is in heaven. (Matt. 5:16)

> For I know the plans I have for you, says the Lord, plans to help you and not hurt you, plans to give you a hope and a future. (Jer. 29:11)

> And the LORD answered me, and said, Write the vision, and make it plain upon tables, that he may run that readeth it. For the vision is yet for an appointed time, but at the end it shall speak, and not lie: though it tarry, wait for it; because it will surely come, it will not tarry. Write the vision for it is for a set time that those who read it may run with it. (Hab. 2:2-3 KJV)

Nurturing Your Family

Ephesians 6:4 says parents are to raise their children in the nurture and admonition of the Lord. This simply means parents are to bring their children up in the training and instruction of the Lord. You and your children must walk in godly ways in order to have God's blessings.

Deuteronomy 28 details the good plan that God has for your family. It is a plan that is good, to give you a hope and a future (Jer. 29:11). Deuteronomy 28 also details the negative plan that rebellion against God will produce in your family.

Parents are to do everything they can to teach their children about God and His ways. When parents train their children in godly ways, the children will know how to sustain relationships. Training in the educational arena is wonderful and parents should do everything they can to give their children proper education. But education alone will not teach our children how to sustain relationships. A person can be a genius and still fail in interpersonal relationships.

All of the Ten Commandments, as well as the whole Bible, are written to help people live right with God and live right with people. It is not one or the other. It is both; live right with God and with people.

Parental Obedience Helps Keep the Family Together

We have looked at the cursed behaviors that cause family disunity in previous chapters and it has been noted what not to do, but it cannot be stressed enough that parents must obey God if they want unity with their children.

Let's look at the life of Abraham. God told him to leave his father's family and go to the place He wanted him to go (Gen. 12:1). God had told Abraham's father to go to that same place years earlier, but he did not go (Gen. 11:31). What if Abraham's father would have obeyed? What if Abraham's father would have done what God told him to do?

If Abraham's father would have obeyed, maybe Abraham would have had Isaac sooner. Maybe Abraham would have been able to put the plan of God in motion sooner. Parental disobedience will hinder children from being trained up in the nurture and admonition of the Lord as soon as the children could. Parental disobedience will hinder how fast their children will be in the plan of God.

This is not to condemn parents for disobedience, but we can see what time is wasted when we as parents do not follow the will of God. In Abraham's family line, we know that Abraham obeyed God. Then Abraham begat Isaac (Gen. 21:3). Isaac never went away from home (Gen. 25:6). No time wasted. Then Isaac begat Jacob and Esau (Gen. 25:25-26). Isaac did not obey God. Jacob went away. Many times we only see that Jacob went away because his life was in danger after his mother helped him steal his brother's blessing (Gen. 27:42-43). However, it had been prophesied that the older would serve the younger (Gen. 25:23). God's plan was the older would serve the younger. Isaac disobeyed God when he planned to bless Esau, who was older. Years would pass before Isaac would see Jacob (the younger) again. Time...

Ecclesiastes 3:1-2 NKJV says, "To everything there is a season. A time for every purpose under heaven: A time to be born and a time to die." Children are born into this world with preset generational blessings and preset generational curses. They come into the world with a preset destiny. God has a plan for them from the foundation of the world. They can be in the plan of God at a young age. He gives them parents to help them understand His plan at a young age.

Everyone Is Commanded to Honor Their Parents

If parents have settled in their hearts to obey God, they will have an easier time teaching their children the plan of God as spelled out in the Bible. God planned for children to honor their parents so that children will have a good life. Even if one of your parents or both of your parents are deceased or for another reason your parents are not in your life, you can still honor them. The Israelites called God, "the God of Abraham, Isaac and Jacob" (Ex. 3:15). Abraham, Isaac and Jacob were long dead, but their memory wasn't. God was called upon to remember the covenant He made with their "fathers."

Before my father passed away he and I didn't see each other very often, yet I was and still am Russell's daughter. I still honor him with my lifestyle. Some people do not know their fathers at all. They can still honor the "office" of father. They can still respect their father for giving them life.

Many people want to believe they are living to themselves. When I attended a celebration for one of my uncle's 50-year wedding anniversary I got a revelation that parents' names go on even after they have died. Isn't that wonderful to have stayed in a unified state for over 50 years? Yes, it is and in the program's bulletin there was a "thank you" to my Grandma Rosa (my mother and uncle's mother). She was being honored although she had died many years before.

Although I'll talk more about how to honor older parents in a later chapter, it will suffice for me to say your life is not your own. Although some people believe they are living their lives in spite of their parents, the truth is all of us are living a life directly influenced by our parents. All of us are living our lives today, right now, based on whether we honored our parents or cursed them.

Respect Comes From the Heart

Honor does not just mean obedience. A child can be obedient without honoring their parents. I have seen my children do what they were told to with such a bad attitude that I almost wished I had not told them to do it. They obeyed me, yet they did not honor me. Again, even though honor includes obedience for young children, honor is respect.

Children are to respect their parents. I asked my son when he was five years old, "What does honor mean?" He said it means to "learn from your parents." That is a good definition. My definition expounds on what Andrew said it means. My definition as it relates in the parent-child relationship is that young children are to learn to obey with a good attitude and adult children are to relate to their parents with a good attitude.

The key to staying rightly-related to others is keeping a good attitude. We have all seen people with a "bad attitude." We can remember when we last displayed one. A good attitude comes from a good heart (Matt. 12:35). It is not manufactured. It is sincere. In order to have a good attitude, a person must be sincere. Sincerity cannot be faked. It is one of those attributes that either you have it or you don't. The whole idea behind the "rolling eyes" is to display insincerity. As parents age, adult children need to make sure that they sincerely honor their parents.

At every age, children are to honor their parents. Babies can even honor their parents. When babies can do things on purpose they should be taught to honor their parents. One time I was talking with a friend and she had on a hat with sunglasses on the hat. She was holding her 7- or 8-month-old son and he kept trying to pull off her hat. It was quite comical. He was pulling the hat, but the mother was trying to keep it on. You can imagine what that was doing to her hair. The point is he was doing it on purpose, but she was not training him to respect her. Honor is usually not an issue until the idea of submission is encountered. With adult children, honor is usually not an issue until an area of disagreement comes up. Adults and children need to speak with a respectful tone to their parents.

Children must be trained to speak respectfully even when they are angry. Unfortunately, according to D. Ross Campbell, author of *How to Really Love Your Child*, most children cannot really handle their anger until they are about 16 or 17 years old. So disrespect can be expected from young children. I am not saying disrespect should be ignored until the children are more mature. I am saying don't allow your child's negativism to overwhelm you when they disrespect you. First Corinthians 13:11 says, "When I was a child, I spoke like a child." Children will speak like children. The good news is a child's ability to articulate his feelings in a respectful tone will increase as his age does.

Parents, begin to train your children at an early age how to relate to you in a positive manner. God chose Abraham because he would train his children. One problem with adult child-parent relationships is that the parent is still trying to train their adult child the same way they did when the adult child was a child. We must remember to treat our adult children like adults. Holding on too long can cause your child to become angry with you.

Stand Up! Everybody, Stand Up!

Adult children should be able to stand without their parents propping them up. Do you remember when your child was a baby and in order for her to sit up, she had to be propped up? Adult children need to know who they are that they might stand un-propped.

My mother told one of my brothers about a vision she once had of him. The vision detailed him and her being attached with a long umbilical cord. The Lord said to her to cut it. This was a vision about a 40-year old son. At birth the umbilical cord is supposed to be cut, but apparently Mother had not let go. Although my brother thought mother talked to him like he was a child, neither one of them was conscious that Mother was still carrying him in her heart like a baby. When Mother "cut" the umbilical cord, Greg's life began to have new meaning.

What does it mean to cut a spiritual umbilical cord? Well, what does it mean in the natural? It means it is time to allow that child to part from you. It means it is time to allow that child to live on his own. Obviously, when a newborn's cord is cut we do not expect that baby to not need us anymore. We don't say to a newborn, "Go on. I carried you for nine months. Go on. You can do it!" No, we don't do that. Yet when you cut a newborn's cord that baby is beginning his life apart from you.

Part of the curse of disunity is that your children do not grow up. Although physical weaknesses are part of the curse, I don't mean they will be physically dependent on you. I mean they will be emotionally and spiritually dependent on you. There are some very immature people in this world. Again, by immature I mean they do not behave like a grown up or they are underdeveloped in the area of relationships.

People who dishonor their parents are immature. People who cannot maintain relationships are underdeveloped in love, nourishment and nurture. They are immature. When children are nurtured spiritually, they grow up. They can stand. It is a blessing to have grown children who can relate to others properly. It is a blessing to see your children relating well to a spouse and grandchildren. My husband and I want our children to grow up. We want them to mature. Although many women are waiting later in life to become mothers, no one wants a 40-year-old baby.

Parents share in the responsibility to see that their children grow up. Parents are not totally responsible because children have to choose to grow up. Many of us heard our parents say, "I didn't raise you that way." The parents' responsibility lies in the training.

Children start training at a young age with good education, activities, and accountability. However, the greatest training we can give to our children, whether they are old or young, will be on how to spiritually stand. Although I am a grown woman with three children of my own, my mother still gives me books and tapes to help me stand in my walk with God.

Co-Dependents Do Not Stand

As I am strong in my relationship with God, I will be rightly-related to the people around me. Many people in today's society are overly dependent, or co-dependent on others. They do not know how to stand on their own financially, emotionally, or spiritually. The welfare system in America has done a disservice to many people by allowing them to use the system too long. This is not a case against welfare. Welfare can be an excellent tool to help poor people survive when they find themselves in hard times. However, when people use welfare as a crutch, they don't intend to take care of themselves. They are co-dependent.

Gambling has the same effect as welfare with the exception that you pay to play. People who gamble are co-dependent. They are co-dependent on the need to "take" other people's money. They are not trusting God to meet their needs. They are not trusting God to give them a good life. They feel they have to take it. Remember, the love of money is the root of all evil (I Tim. 6:10).

The amount of money we have or don't have can sometimes hinder us from fulfilling the plan of God for our lives. Not having a lot of money can be just as much a crutch as having a lot of money was for the rich young ruler. We can become co-dependent on money as well as people, drugs or alcohol. Anything that you have to have to make it in life is something you have gotten co-dependent on.

Our children are co-dependent on us if we are their source for living. If one or both of your parents have died, let me say, I know you really miss them. Let me also ask you, did they teach you how to stand? Did they teach you to put God first? If they did, although you were shaken, you were not utterly cast down (Heb. 12:27). You were able to stand even after they died. If they didn't teach you to stand, you may be still grieving. You may be sad during holidays or special events.

We are only to be dependent on God (Ex. 22:2). Many times we read about the Lord testing people to see if they really were only depending on Him (Gen. 22:12). We are tested in life to see if we are depending only on Him. The greatest commandment is to love the Lord God with all of your heart and all of your soul and all of your strength (Deut. 6:5). We are to be co-dependent on Him. We really can't make it without Him.

Most Christians can embrace the first commandment to love the Lord. They can see how much He has done for them. The second greatest command sometimes (many times) gives people a little trouble (Lev. 19:18). Although we are to love our neighbors as ourselves, we are not to become co-dependent on other people.

Some people confuse love with co-dependence. I have made it a point to define love to my children as a feeling you can only have towards another person (or a pet) who can love you back. Children can "love" candy. They can "love" their bike. But those things cannot love them back. Many times people love people who do not love them back because they have a weak ability to recognize real love. "Loving" inanimate objects weakens your ability to recognize real love from a person.

A co-dependent relationship will be one that you are not loved back because a co-dependent relationship is not a loving relationship. It is a lust-filled relationship. Although we discussed the difference between love and lust in the first chapter, it will suffice to say lust causes us to want love in unhealthy ways. Again, many people confuse lust with love.

__People Confused About Love Do Not Stand__

Many people lust after cars. Cars cannot love you back. Many people lust after houses. Houses cannot love you back. Inanimate things cannot love you. People love you back. God loved you first.

My husband and I did not teach our children to believe that Santa Claus, the Easter Bunny or the Tooth Fairy ever gave them anything. Those icons are based on fictitious love. They are based on fictitious caring. Fictitious characters do not love your children. Fictitious characters are not real.

The argument could be made for St. Nick that he was a real person. He lived many years ago and he loved children. Today, however, parents are the people behind the giving of toys. Parents also give the eggs or money on the other occasions as well. Fictitious characters are getting credit for the parents' love. Parents should get the credit in their child's mind for parental love. When children are older parents want all the credit for the things they have done for their children. Some children are not as grateful as they should be because the parents gave some of their credits away to fictitious characters when the children were young.

Fictitious characters will not help a child when tragedy strikes her family. Fictitious characters cannot physically meet your child's needs. I know many parents who give their young children a "comfort" toy, blanket, even a pacifier. Again, I am not against using those things in a very young child's life. However, I do caution against prolonged usage of such items. I believe when children have comfort items too long those items can become idols. Those things do not have the ability to care about your children.

Ultimately, fictitious love can confuse children about the real love of God. Fictitious love trains children to receive comfort from something that is not real, or is imagined. Although we can't see God, He is not imaginary. He speaks. Our children can really know God (I Sam. 3:1-18).

Our children can experience God's love. He is the one who helps them through times of grief even though He can't be seen. He is the one who provides for their physical needs even though He can't be seen. He is real even though He can't be seen.

Undisciplined Children Do Not Stand

In order for your children to stand, they must not be confused about God's love for them. They must not be confused about your love for them. Although confusion can occur through fictitious love, it occurs most likely during times of discipline. Many parents are unaware that the goal of discipline is to have a wise child.

There are two groups of people who receive a lot of attention in the Bible: the wise and the fool. When our children walk in the wisdom of God, they will stand. When our children walk in foolishness, they will fall. When you discipline your children remind yourself of your goal: to raise a wise child and not a fool. Jesus said in Matthew 7:24-27 (KJV):

"Therefore whosoever heareth these sayings of mine, and doeth them, I will liken him unto a wise man, which built his house upon a rock:

And the rain descended, and the floods came, and the winds blew, and beat upon that house; and it fell not: for it was founded upon a rock.

And every one that heareth these sayings of mine, and doeth them not, shall be likened unto a foolish man, which built his house upon the sand:

And the rain descended, and the floods came, and the winds blew, and beat upon that house; and it fell: and great was the fall of it."

We discipline our children to hear what we say and do what we say. We train them to hear what we say and then do it. A wise child will listen to his parents. A foolish child will not.

If your child is not obeying you, don't ignore his disobedience. That is not to say you vent your anger on him. Venting does not produce obedient children. It produces fearful children. When you discipline your son make sure the consequence fits the disobedience.

Since God corrects us, we do not want our child to grow up being deaf to correction. As we train our children to be wise we are also training them to be humble. Hebrews 12:6 says those the Father loves He chastens. When God told Cain to leave his family, Cain complained the punishment was more than he could bear. But had Cain wisely and humbly heeded God's earlier correction, that level of punishment would not have been necessary.

If your child is characteristically obedient and randomly disobeys, don't ignore his obedient nature. We must guard our hearts from allowing offenses to build up in our minds against our children. This can cause us to treat our children harshly. Our child may be generally very obedient, but an offensive behavior could cause you to think of your generally wise child as an overall foolish child. Again, forgive your children as often as they need to be forgiven. Notice, I didn't say as often as they deserve to be forgiven. Forgiveness is not based on deservedness. Forgiveness is based on need.

As I have mentioned before, the punishment should fit the disobedience, and forgiveness must always be given. You do not want to treat children harshly. You do not want to wound your child's spirit. A child is the most often wounded during harsh times of discipline. I do not mean just corporal punishment. Discipline is not just spanking. Discipline is nurturing and instructing your child. You can harshly instruct your child or you can gently instruct your child. You can grab your Bible out of a toddler's hand or you can ask that toddler to give it to you. Instead of yelling, "I said, NO!", you could firmly say, "I said, no."

There is a big difference between being firm and being harsh. The difference will be whether or not the parent is angry when he disciplines. Remember, anger is not only displayed by yelling. It could also be expressed as irritation, frustration or impatience. Parents who angrily discipline their children wound their children. They may or may not physically wound them, but they will always wound them emotionally and spiritually. When we talk harshly to our children, we wound their spirits.

Brokenhearted Children Do Not Stand Very Well

Psalms 127:4 says a child is "as an arrow in the hand of a warrior." Children will go where you lead them. Many parents are disappointed in their children, but the children are simply going where they were led. My children are going to go where my husband and I lead them. There came a point in my life that I had to look seriously at how I was handling my anger. In my heart, I want to lead my children to the prosperous life of unity. However, if I mishandle my anger I will lead my children to the cursed life of disunity.

Have you looked seriously at how you are handling your anger? Have you looked at where you are leading your children? Maybe your children are grown. Have you led them on the path of unity? Are they on the path of disunity? How would you know if they were on the path of unity? The answer is they peacefully get along with you.

Maybe you came from a home where the family members did not get along. Maybe you came from a broken "heart" home. I call it a broken "heart" home because when homes are broken, it is not necessarily the physical home that is broken. It is more that the hearts of the fathers, mothers and children are broken. Broken hearts lead to disunity. Whole hearts lead to unity.

I believe many people who get married want to be unified with the person they are going to marry. However, they don't understand that they must have a whole heart to be unified with their mate. Unity equals wholeness. No cracks.

The Principles of Unity are a Healing Balm

Early in my marriage, I realized that my heart was not whole. I might just add: even under the best relationships there is a strain on the heart as you and your partner become one. Still, whole-hearted people will be able to maintain their marriages. Whole-hearted people will want to sustain their marriages. The good news is that God healed my heart. My husband and I have been able to maintain our marriage for over ten years. We want to sustain our marriage until death parts us. God is no respecter of persons (Acts 10:34). He can do the same for you as He has done for us.

My husband was instrumental to my healing. He accepted me. He encouraged my spiritual growth. He even fed me. (He is a great cook.) Yet he could not heal my heart. Only God could make my heart whole so that I would want to withstand the pressure of being a wife. There is pressure in life and the pressure can be so great that it rips your family apart. Philippians 2:13 says that God works in us to do His will and to want His good pleasure. It is His good pleasure to strengthen us to withstand the pressures of life.

I came from a home where the pressure of life could not be withstood. I came from a broken "heart" home. I didn't realize that my heart was broken until I tried to be unified with my husband. We didn't have big fights or yelling matches. Still, neither he nor I could understand why we could not develop the deep intimacy we knew we needed to have a good marriage. We thought idealized love was all we needed. The longer we were married the more we realized we needed biblical love.

Biblical love is expressed as described in First Corinthians 13. Biblical love values others and treats them in a positive manner. Biblical love will sustain a marriage.

Love is a matter of the heart and no matter what the age is of the couple, their love will always be a matter of their hearts. My parents divorced in their 30s and neither my father nor my mother remarried. I could have easily followed my parents in disunity. I could have divorced and been perpetually single. If God had not stepped in our lives to show us His love, my husband and I would have easily been a statistic. Not because we didn't love each other. Not because we didn't believe in marriage. Both of our hearts had been broken (my husband's heart had been broken when his mother died suddenly when he was in college) and they could not be taped up. They must be healed. They must be made whole.

Love many times is used as the "magic" tape to cover broken hearts. We want to put love over our wounded hearts and say, "All better." One time my daughter ripped one of my son's art papers. He was sad. I simply taped it back together and it was all better. He was happy. My heart is not paper. Your heart is not paper. When it gets ripped, it must be healed. Love is supposed to flow from inside the heart to the outside, not from outside of the heart to within the heart.

In the beginning of our marriage, my husband loved me. He was patient. He could see that something was wrong, but he could not fix it. I want to say again. Your spouse cannot heal your heart. Many people put pressure on their spouses to make them feel better. Many people try to make their spouses feel that if they loved them more the relationship would be better. Although the relationship will improve when the spouses are more selfless, more understanding and more peaceful, someone with a broken heart will never be satisfied. In order to be a satisfied person you must have a whole heart.

God is the only one who can heal your heart (Ex. 15:26). God is who healed my heart. As I received the love, nourishment and nurture of God, my heart was healed. Healing is something to be received. When you are sick in your body, in order to be well, you receive medicine or you receive a supernatural healing touch from God. It is nothing that you do. You cannot heal yourself. Other relationships will not heal your heart. Only God can heal your heart.

When God heals your heart He doesn't just pour on love. He pours on love, nourishment and nurture with the goal of you pouring it into others. Perhaps you were not nurtured in the ways of God, and you did not realize how much your life depended on having long-lasting, meaningful relationships. It's not too late. God has a good plan for your life and it includes how to relate to other people in a godly way. When we relate to others in a godly way, we will be standing for God.

God Supplies the Strength to Stand

When our children have whole hearts they will stand for God. When our children have on the full of armor of God, they will have the spiritual strength to stand in their walks with God. They will be trained to depend on God. They will be trained to live for God. Ephesians 6:1:9 says:

> Children, obey your parents in the Lord: for this is right.
> Honour thy father and mother; (which is the first commandment with promise;)
> That it may be well with thee, and thou mayest live long on the earth.

And, ye fathers, provoke not your children to wrath: but bring them up in the nurture and admonition of the Lord.

Servants, be obedient to them that are your masters according to the flesh, with fear and trembling, in singleness of your heart, as unto Christ;

Not with eyeservice, as menpleasers; but as the servants of Christ, doing the will of God from the heart;

With good will doing service, as to the Lord, and not to men:

Knowing that whatsoever good thing any man doeth, the same shall he receive of the Lord, whether he be bond or free.

And, ye masters, do the same things unto them, forbearing threatening: knowing that your Master also is in heaven; neither is there respect of persons with him.

The first nine verses of tells us about divine order because without submission, the armor will not work. The armor does not work if one is living in disobedience, yet it will work for anyone, child or adult, who is living with a submissive, humble attitude. Ephesians 6:10-18 (KJV) encourages us to put on the armor of God.

Finally, my brethren, be strong in the Lord, and in the power of his might.

Put on the whole armour of God, that ye may be able to stand against the wiles of the devil.

For we wrestle not against flesh and blood, but against principalities, against powers, against the rulers of the darkness of this world, against spiritual wickedness in high places.

Remember, although we want to walk in unity, the enemy will try to prevent us from maintaining unity in our families. It may be your father yelling at you, but it is the devil trying to discourage you from your goal. It may be your child slamming her bedroom door, but is the devil trying to keep you from reaching your goal. He will send circumstances and events to try to distract you from your goal of unity. Remember, the trap!

> **Wherefore take unto you the whole armour of God, that ye may be able to withstand in the evil day, and having done all, to stand.**
> **Stand** therefore, having your loins girt about with truth, and having on the breastplate of righteousness;
> And your feet shod with the preparation of the gospel of peace;
> Above all, taking the shield of faith, wherewith ye shall be able to quench all the fiery darts of the wicked.
> And take the helmet of salvation, and the sword of the Spirit, which is the word of God:
> Praying always with all prayer and supplication in the Spirit, and watching thereunto with all perseverance and supplication for all saints;

You can stand for unity if you are a truthful person. You can stand for unity if you receive love, nourishment and nurture from God. You can stand for unity if you give love, nourishment and nurture to others. You can stand for unity if you are able to share the gospel with others. You can stand for unity if you can recognize confusing behaviors, selfish ambitions and unrighteous anger. You can stand for unity if you are sure of your salvation. You can stand for unity if you read your Bible. You can stand for unity if you pray for your family. You can stand for unity if you keep on the armor of God.

We Must Keep On the Armor of God

When we wound our children's spirits they put down their armor. Proverbs 18:14 says, "The spirit of a man will sustain his infirmity; but a wounded spirit who can bear?" Psalms 106:32-33 says, "The people angered him also at the waters of strife, so that it went ill with Moses for their sakes: Because they provoked his spirit, so that he spake unadvisedly with his lips." Moses did something foolish when the people strove with him. He put down his spiritual armor. Moses was not a fool. Moses was wise, but when he got angry he put down his armor.

The armor of God is spiritual armor. My son has an armor of God play set. There is a helmet, a belt, a breastplate, a shield, a sword, two shin guards for the legs. It gives him a natural example of the armor. But the "of God" part is supernatural. It is spiritual. Ephesians 6:4 tells parents not to provoke their children's spirits. When we provoke our children we provoke them spiritually, not just naturally. When we provoke our children we strive with them and then they believe they have an excuse to do something foolish.

The Bible says Moses spoke unadvisedly. One of the ways you can tell a person has put down their armor is to listen to what they say about their parents. People who have a good report about their parents attract people who have a good report about their parents. Many parents pray for their children's future mates. Yet if that child murmurs and complains and always finds fault with her parents that child will not attract a person who has a good relationship with his parents. Generally, a person who is angry with her parents will not attract a person who has a good relationship with his parents.

I say generally because there are examples of someone from a good background who marries someone from an angry background and the marriage works. Still, a lot of anger will have to be worked out in order for that marriage to be a good marriage.

Good relationships are not accidental. They are not based on "magical" love. Good relationships are based on low anger levels. Having a good relationship with your children is based on you not angrily disciplining them. People are often deceived to think that anger will produce a good relationship with their children. Some parents use anger to try to control their children. Having control does not mean that you will have a good relationship with your children.

Some people give their children too much control out of fear of hurting their children. They just try to maintain a friendship with their children. Parents are more than friends to their children and yet they are still to be friends. Parents are called to have a good relationship with their children.

Unrighteous anger separates people. Remember, it is not a sin for you to get angry with your child or for your child to get angry with you. God gave everyone the emotion of anger. However, it is a sin for you to use your anger against your children and it is a sin for your children to use their anger against you. As I said earlier, anger is a legitimate emotion and it should be used for justice. We should feel angry about unfair treatment. We should feel angry when our children disobey us, but we should not try to make them "pay" for their disobedience. We want wise children. When anger is used for revenge it will be very destructive. It will wound the spirit. It will hurt the heart.

As I have mentioned, hurting people hurt people. It can also be said angry people anger people. Anger is transferable (Prov. 22:24-25). If I take my anger out on my son, he will take his anger out on me by being angry at me and pass on the generational curse of disunity when he grows up by being angry at his son, my grandson. Either way it comes back to me. Proverbs 15:20 says a foolish son hurts his mother. But be sure foolish mothers and fathers can produce foolish children.

Proverbs 22:15 says foolishness is bound up in the heart of a child, but the rod of correction will drive it out. Parents are to drive foolishness out of their children with correction. It is up to fathers and mothers to train their children to be wise. Training a child is not quick. Think of the times when you were potty training your child. You made him go to the potty over and over until one day he went on his own.

Re-Training Is Available

Training means to instruct so as to make someone proficient or qualified. When someone is in training, she will do something over and over until she is good at it. In the military the recruits are forced to do certain drills over and over until they can do them instinctively. One day that training could be used to save their lives. When we train our children about how to deal with their anger wisely, one day that training could to be used to save them from foolishly using their anger against you or someone else. The earlier you start training your child to correctly and righteously handle their anger, the longer your children will be able to walk free from the curse of disunity.

If your children are grown and have not learned to handle their anger, they are probably walking in the curse of disunity. All divorces are caused by the curse of disunity. All separations are caused by the curse of disunity. All runaway children ran because of the curse of disunity. Anger is the major problem in every family where people are not getting along.

There is still hope. Angry behaviors are learned behaviors. They can be unlearned. Even if your child is grown, you can still model the correct way to handle anger. All angry episodes should end in resolution. Ephesians 4:26 says we are not to let our anger go until the next day. Clear the air. Seek resolution. Always seek restoration in your relationships.

In the case of abuse many relationships will not be restored. The hardheartedness of some people makes it necessary for families to part ways. When marriages end in divorce, whether abuse was an issue or not, the hearts of parents and the children must be healed. Healing takes place in your heart when you feel accepted and valued (love), know your purpose for being on this earth (nourishment) and are trained to stand for God (nurture).

Many people get into bad relationships because of lack in one of the three areas of unity, or the curse of disunity. Your parents were supposed to train you in the principles of unity. If they didn't, I want to stand in the gap for your parents right now. Maybe you were abused as a child. Maybe you were neglected as a child. Maybe you were not taught to stand. Allow me right now as a parent to say, "I am sorry. I was wrong. Please forgive me. Don't stay angry with me. I love you. God has a good plan for your life. Don't stop believing in Him. Be healed." Even as you read this, see these words coming out of your father's or mother's mouth.

I want you to be healed. God wants you to be healed. Your children need you to be healed. Allow your soul to be healed and you will live in the blessing of unity with your children.

Here are a few godly ways to nurture your family members:

1. Participate in a family devotion. Family devotions give parents an excellent opportunity to ensure that their children understand the Bible and biblical principles.
2. Memorize scriptures. As soon as a child can talk, she can begin to quote scriptures. Psalms 119:11 says, "Thy Word have I hid in my heart that I might not sin against Thee." My children have been quoting Philippians 4:13, "I can do all things through Christ who strengthens me" since they were toddlers.
3. Talk to your family about the healing power of God. Some denominations teach that healing is not for today. Acts 10:38 says that Jesus went about doing good and healed all who were oppressed by the devil. Jesus still lives and He still heals.
4. Give your family members videos and books about Christian character. There is so much on the market today to increase the knowledge of God in a young person's or adult's life. Take advantage of living in the Information Age.
5. Repent to your family members when you mishandle your anger. This will train your children to do likewise.

The purpose of nurturing your family members is to make them strong in the Lord. The purpose of nurturing your family members is to give them the ability to stand for God. The purpose of nurturing your family members is to help them stand for unity. Train your children up in the way they shall go and they will not depart from it (Prov. 22:6).

God's Word to on how to Stand:

Be strong in the Lord and in the power of His might. (Ephesians 6:10)

Fear ye not, stand still, and see the salvation of the Lord. (Ex. 14:13 KJV)

Casting down imaginations, and every high thing that exalteth itself against the knowledge of God, and bringing into captivity every thought to the obedience of Christ. (II Corinthians 10:5 KJV)

You shall love the LORD your God with all your heart, with all your soul, and with all your strength. (Deut. 6:5 KJV)

Honoring the Senior Generation

As I have said before, to honor your father and mother is not just a commandment to young children. It is a commandment to all children. As adult children we honor our parents by loving, nurturing and nourishing them. Adults need love, nurturing and nourishment as much as children do. And particularly as adult children, we can show our parents great honor.

In Okinawa, Japan, many people live to be in their 100's and the younger people there truly honor their great age. Joyce Meyer has a beautiful testimony of honoring her parents. Her parents mistreated her while she was growing up. She was abused by her dad. But in spite of that, God taught her how to really love her parents and I believe He abundantly blessed her for honoring her parents.

Many older people are not honored in their old age. Just as many people systematically put their children in daycare centers, many seniors are being systemically put in nursing homes. Just as there are many great daycare centers, there are many great nursing homes. But be mindful not to forget your senior parents. God has blessed us to be a blessing to our parents, especially through their senior years.

Someone who worked in a nursing home once told me that you could really tell the families where the parents had good relationships with their children. The children came to visit them. Children will not come to visit when there is a bad relationship. Don't be deceived and think that as your children mature that if your children don't visit you that everything is all right. Everything is not all right. There is a curse of disunity operating in your family.

I recently met a woman who said she had not seen her mother in eight years. Because America has such an easy transportation system, there is only one reason she did not see her mother. It was because she didn't want to. Isn't that a harsh reality? She didn't want to see her mother. For some reason that daughter did not receive love, nourishing or nurturing from her mother. Again, children either go away to break the curse from their parents or they go away to help others break the curse from their parents. If the children go away to help others break the curse, they will maintain a good relationship with their parents. The curse of disunity is the result of having a bad relationship with parents.

Your Parents Want You to Take Care of Your Children

To honor your senior parents, there are also people you should love, nourish and nurture on their behalf. The first group is your children. Most grandparents adore their grandchildren. By loving, nurturing and nourishing your children, you will honor your parents. Many people who do not take care of their children are unaware that they are doing it to spite their parents.

I once heard of a parent saying, "Why is my child doing me this way?" That person was taking their child's "bad" behavior personally. There are some things in life you don't take personally, but your relationship with your children should be taken personally.

Your relationship with your parents should be taken personally. Your life is a reflection of your parents. Your ability to sustain yourself is a reflection of your relationship with your parents. You could say, "I can't help that I am poor." Actually, you can. If you are a child of God, God has blessed you so that you can be a blessing. There is no excuse for neglecting, underfeeding, or abusing your children. The principles in this book have been laid out so that you can care for your children and honor your parents.

The Bible says that anything that you really want you can have (Mark 11:24). The point is you must really want it. You must really want to be a great parent. You must really want to raise great children. You must really want to honor your parents. When you honor your parents it will be well with you. When you dishonor your parents it will not be well with you.

Illness (being not well) can take many forms. It can be in a person's body, but it can also be in a person's finances and in relationships. Illness is part of the curse. If you are motivated to break the curse, you will instill in yourself and your children the attitude of healthy (very well) me. In God's eyes, when we are healthy inside of our hearts we can receive all the promises of prosperity that the Bible promises us (III Jn. 2). God promises to bless us liberally in finances, health and relationships.

God has given you every provision for your children (Ps. 112:2). He has provided the fruit of the Spirit for your attitude (Gal. 5:22-23). He has provided good education and all kinds of lessons for your child to learn (Ps. 32:8). He has provided all kinds of good nutritious food for them to eat (Ps. 103:5). He has even provided the path and the plan for their lives (Prov. 4:18). The main sacrifice of parents is to make sure our children have everything God has provided for them. When we take care of our children we honor God and our parents.

Proverbs 17:6 says children's children are the crown of old men. Your parents want you to be good to your children. Your parents want you to treat your children like they are special to you. Many times grandparents will go out of their way to be a blessing to your children. I know of a family at my church whose children attended our church's privately-owned Christian school. They only had a little money, but they believed God to provide a way for their children to go to Christian school. God made a way through the dad's parents. The paternal grandparents paid for one year's tuition. What a blessing that was to that family! As we do what we can for our children, often grandparents will do the extra that we can't do or are having a hard time doing.

Some Grandparents Raise Their Grandchildren

There are many instances when grandparents have to do the job of parents and take care of their grandchildren. I heard of a 70-year-old woman who was considering rearing her three-year-old grand-child because her son was mentally unstable and seemed unable to do it. You wouldn't think that someone in her 70's should have to raise such a young child. I don't know how long the curse had been operating in this woman's life before the grandchild came along, but it probably was a long time.

Of grandparents who rear their grandchildren, I believe these grandparents are getting a second chance with their grandchildren that they missed with their children. Most grandparents can see what they did wrong with their children. Most grandparents are more emotionally stable than they were when they were raising their children. As a result, many times children raised by grandparents have a more mature demeanor than children their own age who are being raised by their parents.

Samuel was taken care of by a grandparent. Eli wasn't Samuel's grandparent, yet Eli was a grandparent. Eli had a second chance to raise up godly seed with Samuel when he would not restrain his own children. When Eli realized that God was calling Samuel, he knew how to guide Samuel in the things of God. Samuel listened to Eli whereas Eli's own sons did not listen to him. One day Israel would follow the word of Samuel. Eli's own family would be cut off.

Samuel's story is such a touching part of the Bible. Samuel's mother, Hannah, was barren for many years. Then she prayed for a child and conceived Samuel. After Samuel was born Hannah and her husband lent Samuel to the Lord. They left him with Eli to do the work of the ministry. (I Sam. 1) The Bible says Samuel was a boy wearing a linen ephod (I Sam. 2:18). The ephod was reserved for priests. According to Exodus 39:2-7 NLT:

The ephod was made from fine linen cloth and embroidered with gold thread and blue, purple, and scarlet yarn. A skilled craftsman made gold thread by beating gold into thin sheets and cutting it into fine strips. He then embroidered it into the linen with the blue, purple, and scarlet yarn.

It was very significant for a child to wear a linen ephod. In those times, wearing linen represented the priestly role, royalty and righteousness. When grandchildren have godly grandparents raising them, they are like children wearing linen ephods. They have a special grace upon their lives. They have a special sensitivity to people. They have to understand at a young age that their parents can't take care of them.

In the natural, Samuel's parents appeared to be able to raise Samuel. Yet because the plan of God was so great on his life, it was going to take someone in a high spiritual position to bring it to pass. Eli was the high priest. There was no one higher than Eli. It was going to take Eli to bring out the call that was on Samuel's life.

When God called Samuel, Eli understood the Lord was calling him (I Sam. 3:1-11). In the Old Testament the Lord did not speak to everyone. Today God will speak to anyone who will listen. But God not only wants to speak to people who will listen and respect Him, He also wants to speak to people who will listen and respect their parents. Eli's own sons would not listen and respect him. Therefore, to preserve the "family of Israel" God chose Samuel to be His spokesman instead of Eli's sons, and the Bible says none of Samuel's words fell to the ground (I Sam. 3:19). Children raised by grandparents can preserve the family when their parents will not listen.

Your Parents Want You to Get Along With Your Siblings

Just like God wants Israel to be preserved, He wants your family to be preserved. God preserved Samuel's family. His mother, Hannah, went on to have five other children. Samuel was the oldest of six children. We do not know too much about them, but this brings us to the discussion of the second group of people you are to love, nourish and nurture. Your siblings. I have not discussed siblings much in this book. But this is the time to discuss them. When you get along with your siblings you honor your parents.

Many businesses worldwide are family owned. They are run by parents and siblings. Many family businesses fail when the parents die because the siblings can't get along. Family businesses and families in general are sustained by the siblings getting along. It is true that children (brothers and sisters) are our future.

<u>You, Your Siblings and Your Parents</u>

If you have a good relationship with your siblings, great! Nevertheless, some people resent their brothers and/or sisters, but it all boils down to one or all of the children dishonoring their parents. Cain resented Abel. Cain resented the fact that Abel's offering was more pleasing to God than his offering. Cain felt he was not as acceptable as Abel. Cain killed his brother, his father's and mother's son. Cain did not honor his father and mother.

Joseph's brothers threw him in a pit, sold him as a slave and told their father he was dead. Joseph's brothers were envious of him. They didn't like his dreams, but more than that they didn't like the favor that their father bestowed on Joseph. They didn't like it that their father made Joseph a special coat. They didn't like it that their father would send Joseph to tattle on them. After they sold Joseph into slavery they didn't mind telling their father that his favorite son was dead (Gen. 37:3-35). Can you see that though they took their frustrations out on Joseph their anger was directed toward their dad?

Much of sibling rivalry is misdirected. The child may be acting unmannerly to her sister, yet her goal is to get something from her parents. If children "can't" get their parents to love, nourish and nurture them in a nice way they try to get them to do it in a negative way. This is immature. Children are immature. They are not developed in the area of relationships. Parents should be very sensitive to a child who is acting in a negative way to get attention. That child not only wants something from them, that child also needs something from them. Some people believe that if they withhold love, nourishment or nurture from a child, the child will get tired of wanting it.

When a child is loved, nourished and nurtured he will be a child that is easily satisfied. Personality makes a difference in the amount of love, nourishment and nurture a child will need. The child's personality will determine how hard he will try to get what he needs. Don't mistake a child's quiet demeanor to mean that he is receiving all of the love, nourishment and nurture that he needs. Don't mistake a child's active demeanor that he is receiving too much love, nourishment and nurture.

Every personality needs love and nurturing. The difference between the personalities will show up during nourishing. How much time did the parents spend building up the child's self-esteem? How much time did the parents spend encouraging that child to fulfill God's plan for their lives. A child with poor self-esteem will require much more nourishment than a child with a good self-esteem.

Needs left unfilled become lust. Lust is insatiable. Until that child is loved, nourished and nurtured he will continue to act out. Again, although parents cannot give in to a child's every request, they must be sure to love, nourish and nurture their child. Otherwise, he will grow into an adult with an insatiable desire for attention, who resents his siblings.

Think about the prodigal son's older brother. We don't read about him being upset that his brother was gone. We don't read about him going after his brother to try to dissuade him. We only read about him being upset when his brother came home. The older brother liked having his father all to himself.

Sibling Rivalry Can Hinder Unity

Most competition betweens brothers and/or sisters is innocent. It is a part of life. We all want to be number one. There can be a healthy spurring on to good works if the siblings get along. However, sibling rivalry can be also very hurtful when ill feelings are involved.

Ill feelings such as jealousy, envy, begrudging or covetousness occur earliest in childhood. Two brothers are quietly playing together. Suddenly one pulls out the newest, fastest, greatest toy ever, and after the admiration of the toy a power struggles ensues. "It's mine," yells owner of the toy. "I was only looking at it," his brother shouts back. Is the owner of the toy jealous? Is he being suspicious? Is his brother envious of the owner of the toy? Is the brother begrudging the owner of the toy? Is the brother coveting the owner's toy?

Ill feelings can occur very often during the course of one's life.

Therefore, we must guard our hearts. I feel we must guard ourselves against jealousy the most. Jealousy is an unhealthy suspicious nature.

Jealousy can be provoked by our siblings being envious, begrudging, or covetous toward us. If your sister wants something you have or is not happy that you have it, you can react with jealousy. You feel you must guard it. The only thing we are to guard is our hearts. Satan can plant vain imaginations in our minds and we can wrongly believe that our sisters want something we have or are not happy that we have it and we react with jealousy. We can be actually suspicious of our sisters for no reason.

Humanly speaking, there is never a good reason to be jealous. However, it is good to understand how we come to this state of being and avoid behaving like that. We also need to understand how we become envious, begrudging or covetous and avoid behaving like that.

According to Webster's New World Dictionary, envious feelings are feelings of discontent and ill will because of someone's advantages or possessions. Parents have to beware stirring up envious feelings among their children. The most common way for parents to stir up envy in their children is by playing favorites. By buying one daughter something and not buying the other daughter anything or giving one son more compliments than another son is playing favorites. In essence, loving, nurturing or nourishing one child more than another child is playing favorites.

Children pick up on unfair treatment. While we may not treat our children equally because of the age differences or gender, we should work diligently to treat our children fairly. McDonald's© has sold Happy Meals™ for children for a long time. Although the contents can vary, the basic meal is a hamburger, small fries and milk. In more recent years McDonald's© has sold Mighty Kid Meals™. The Mighty Kid Meal™ has more food than a Happy Meal. These meals differ between young and older children. Remember, as parents we want to treat our children the way they need to be treated, not like an older or younger sibling.

There are times when children will say it isn't fair and it could be fair. They can misunderstand the situation or they may simply want something that is not appropriate for them. Again, it may not be equal, but it still could be fair. At times like that one sibling may be begrudging another sibling. Johnny is simply unwilling that his brother, Jimmy, possesses or enjoys something that Jimmy needs or deserves. The older brother begrudged the prodigal son's right to enjoy his homecoming celebration. Joseph's brothers begrudged Joseph the right to enjoy his coat of many colors. When we criticize our siblings' accomplishments, we begrudge them the right to enjoy their accomplishments.

Many times we are actually coveting our sibling's accomplishments. We wish we could have that. We wish we could do that. Although I have discussed covetousness in a previous chapter, I have not discussed it in the light of sibling rivalry. I previously used the example of my son wanting my French fries. Coveting could also be to want a sibling's clothes, car, house, or lifestyle. Remember, coveting is to want someone else's belongings.

Jealousy, envy, begrudging, and covetousness are serious issues among siblings. Yet these negative emotions are the direct result of a child rating herself lowly when compared with her siblings. Second Corinthians 10:12 says we are not to compare ourselves against anyone. As we discussed in the Nourish Chapter, God has an individual plan for each of our lives. We cannot compare our lives to our siblings because God has a specific plan for them just as He has for us. When we are content with who we are, we will not be mad if our siblings have more than we have and we will not gloat if our siblings have less than we have.

Sibling rivalry can bring bitter experiences to the lives of brothers and sisters. But God's will is for us to get along with our siblings. Luke 6:27-31 (NKJV) says:

> "But I say to you who hear: Love your enemies, do good to those who hate you,
> bless those who curse you, and pray for those who spitefully use you.
> To him who strikes you on the one cheek, offer the other also. And from him who takes away your cloak, do not withhold your tunic either.

Give to everyone who asks of you. And from him who
takes away your goods do not ask them back.

And just as you want men to do to you, you also do to
them likewise."

Who are your enemies? Many people think of a terrorist or
some other villainous personality as their enemy, but the Bible says
enemies can be members of your own household (Matt. 10:36).
Sibling rivalry can be so severe that the siblings seem like enemies.

Ill feelings are not limited to young siblings. Adult siblings can
be jealous, envious, begrudging and covetous of each other. Parents
can harbor these same negative emotions even against their own
children. Parents can jealously guard their possessions, be envious
of their child's possessions, begrudge their child the right to enjoy
his accomplishments or covet something their child has.

Again, jealousy, envy, begrudging, and covetousness are the
direct result of poor self-esteem. Poor self-esteem is the result of
lack. Brothers and sisters who love, nourish, or nurture their siblings
can help build up their siblings' esteem.

Your Family is to be a Community of Peoples

When you walk in unity towards your siblings you will walk in
forgiveness toward them. And remember, unity does not mean that
everything will be perfect all the time. Unity between siblings means
I can forgive my siblings when they hurt my feelings. Unity between
siblings means I allow them to be who they are. This doesn't mean
that we allow our siblings to run over us with their idiosyncrasies
or obsessions. But it does mean we allow our siblings to be unique.
Every one has their own personality. The purpose of coming together
is not to be just like all the other family members. You have to be
you and they have to be them. Unhealthy soul ties prevent family
members from being themselves (see Circle of Unity).

The theme of this book is "keep your family together." It is not
only important to keep your immediate family together, but also
your extended family. All the individual families of a family should
come together. In the Old Testament, God called the whole family of

Israel to come together to holy convocations (Lev. 23:2). Holidays are a great time for families to come together. Family reunions are a great time for families to come together. The purpose of the whole family coming together is for the whole family to walk in unity. When our families walk in unity there is no limit to what we could accomplish for God (Ps. 133:1-3).

God's plan is for families to accomplish His will. Christian families are supposed to have dominion over the earth (Gen. 1:26). We are supposed to be communities of peoples (Gen. 28:3). Most communities are self-sufficient. In the community of Tulsa where I live, there is a grocery store, a dentist office, a school, a church, a fire station, a dry cleaner's and many other small businesses. When families come together we learn what kind of people are in our families. Maybe someone is a doctor. Maybe there are educators. When families come together we learn who we are. There is spiritual strength in this kind of unity.

Today many people are lonely. God's answer for loneliness is to put the lonely in families (Ps. 68:6). Some people are in a family, but they are still lonely. Maybe you are the lonely one. Begin to reach out with the principles of love, nourishment and nurture. Don't be afraid. Luke 6:38 says give and it will be given back to you.

You may look back over your life and find a string of broken relationships. The curse of disunity can be broken when you begin to honor your parents. When you treat your children and siblings with respect you will honor your parents.

Be a Witness to Your Parents

You know...your parents won't live forever. Hebrews 9:27 tells us it has been appointed unto a man once to die. Perhaps as you read this your parents have already died. Hopefully, they knew the Lord. If your parents are still living, hopefully they know the Lord.

You should want to know where your parents stand with the Lord. Their eternal future is at stake. Their salvation is at stake.

There are many people who do not believe some portion of what it takes to truly be saved. Some people don't believe that Jesus was the son of God, and you need to believe that in order to be saved.

Some people don't believe that He was really a man, and you need to believe that in order to be saved. Some people simply cannot believe in some aspect of God's goodness. I know of a woman's mother who didn't believe in an aspect of God's goodness. She didn't believe that anyone could know if they would go to heaven or not when they died. The daughter shared with her elderly mother that she could know. A few months later the elderly mother died knowing that she would go to heaven because of her relationship with Christ (Jn. 14:3). The daughter loved her mother and it was comforting to her to know that her mother was present with the Lord (II Cor. 5:8).

The daughter witnessed to her mother for many years before she accepted the truth about God. The daughter doesn't have any regrets. She had settled all issues many years ago. She had a good relationship with her mother and did not grow weary in her well doing (Gal. 6:9).

Have you settled all issues? If your parents die and you have not settled it in your heart to honor them, you will be left with many regrets. Settle every issue you have with your parents. Some parents were abusive. Some were neglectful. Some were poor. Still, they gave you life and it is not God's will that any should perish (II Pet. 3:9). Be a witness unto your parents. Pray for laborers to cross their paths if they are not saved and settle every issue that would prevent you from honoring them.

Maybe your parents did not know how to love, nourish or nurture you, but here you are with this book in your hand, learning these principles of unity. You could teach them to your parents. If you can't teach them to your parents, you can certainly model them for your parents. You can certainly honor your parents.

As young children, we expected our parents to do good things for us. Now that we are adults we can be really good to our parents. Now that we are adults we can really appreciate our parents. Now that we are adults we can really love (value + positive treatment) our parents.

Be good to your parents. Honor your father and mother and it will be well with you.

Cover Your Family

In 2005 Hurricane Katrina hit the Gulf Coast of America and destroyed many homes, businesses, churches, and families. Hurricane Katrina was a natural disaster, but it also illustrated the destroying power of the curse of disunity. During the evacuation for safety, there were many children who were separated from their parents. It was not intentional that those children were separated from their parents. But there was a spiritual reason.

Although children who are placed in foster homes are placed in them intentionally, there is still a spiritual reason why those children are separated from their parents. There are not only natural forces working against children, there are also spiritual forces working against them. It will take prayer to defeat the spiritual forces that empower the curse of disunity.

I have discussed that you can bring unity to your family by passing on the generational blessing of loving, nurturing and nourishing your family. However, not only do we want to accept our family members, not only do we want to strengthen our family members, not only do we want to feed them and feed their vision, but we also want to cover them in prayer. In order for families to walk in unity, some of the people will have to change. In fact, everyone will have to change. In order for families to walk in unity, life cannot go on as it has been. Change must occur, but the motivation to change only occurs through prayer (Prov. 21:1).

Prayer Is Spiritual Warfare

Prayer is a totally spiritual matter. When someone says that he is going to pray, they mean they are going to immerse into the spiritual realm of life. In the Introduction, I discussed the natural, or the soulish, part of our lives. In closing I will discuss the spiritual part of our lives. As I have already mentioned, when God made people He made us in three parts: spirit, soul and body. The spirit of a person is the part that connects him to the spiritual life. The body is the part that connects a person to the earthly life. Yet it is your spirit that keeps you alive on the earth.

When your spirit leaves your body, your earthly life has ended. There are many people who believe in reincarnation. They believe that people never end their earthly lives, but continue to live as something or someone else. This is a false belief. The earthly life does not continue to exist for those who have died. They don't come back as a cow or in another body. Still, when the earthly life ceases, life does not end. Your spirit will live forever. Not in an earthly life, but in eternal life. Everyone's spirit will spend eternity somewhere - either in heaven or in hell.

God intends for our lives to be like heaven on earth (Matt. 6:10).

However, when someone is cursed in their earthly life, their life will seem more like hell. A curse is a demonic spiritual phenomenon. Disunity is not merely a natural phenomenon. Maybe a person is confused about how to love his family members. Maybe he is selfish about his time. Maybe he uses unrighteous anger against their family members. Yet when a person experiences the curse, although the natural life is affected, there is a demonic influence in the spirit affecting the natural life (Prov. 26:2).

Some people do not believe in demons, but that is simply because they have not read their Bible. First John 3:8-9 says, "For this purpose the Son of God was manifested, that He might destroy the works of the devil." Ephesians 6:11 says, "Put on the whole armor of God, that you may be able to stand against the wiles of the devil." James 4:7 says, "Submit to God and resist the devil."

The devil is just as real as God. However, whereas God is true, the devil is a liar. John 8:44 says that he is the father of lies. Satan is a deceiver. He deceived us before we were saved and He could be deceiving your family members right now. His deception causes people to think they can get away with sin. His deception causes people to think they do not have to obey God. It is his deception that causes people to think they do not need God.

The curse has been allowed to operate in some lives because they have not fully surrendered their lives over to God. In the spirit they have given the devil a place (Eph. 4:27). The curse has been allowed to operate in some lives because the people do not know that to spiritually overcome they must stand on God's Word.

In the Chapter on Nurture, I shared with you how to spiritually stand for God. In this chapter I will share with you how to spiritually stand against the devil. We stand against the devil by standing on the truth of God's Word to pull down strongholds, or lies, set up by the devil (II Cor. 10:4).

A stronghold in ancient times was a physical place of defense that people ran into during times of war. A biblical stronghold in modern times is a false defensive system in a person's mind. It is a system of thinking that prevents people from changing. As you pray for change for your family, be aware that some of your family members have strongholds, deceptions of the devil, which will make them unwilling to change. Many people believe the way it is will be the way it always will be. But God says in Isaiah 43:19, "Behold, I will do a new thing, now it shall spring forth, shall ye not know it? I will even make a way in the wilderness, and rivers in the desert." God always changes things for the better (Rom. 8:28).

Change Is Spiritual Warfare

When people do not understand that they are a spirit, they resist change. Even though many people say they want change, they resist changing. They may recognize unity in a family is a good thing, but somehow the necessary change does not come to bring out unity. Something consistently happens to cause disunity. Mothers keep speaking in the same angry tone they have always used. Fathers are just as selfish as they have always been. Children are still disrespectful. Change is not easy and change is usually not instant.

Strongholds must come down before any change will be permanent. Therefore, be prepared for a fight if you want change. The fight, however, is a spiritual fight. Change is God's fight. The early 1960's was a time when African-Americans and many Caucasians wanted change. Martin Luther King, Jr. rose up as a leader because he knew the fight for change was a spiritual fight. He encouraged peace marches. There were others who also wanted change, but they thought change was a physical fight. They encouraged riots. Both parties wanted the same thing. They both wanted change. But when people do not understand that change is a spiritual fight between spiritual beings, they will try to do intellectual or physical warfare when only spiritual warfare will do.

Ephesians 1:18 says the eyes of our understanding must be opened in order for us to be able to spiritually see. The "eyes of understanding" are our spiritual eyes. We have natural eyes, but spiritual things are not naturally discerned (I Cor. 2:14). Although some people have open visions, in which they see something in the future with their eyes open, people cannot see in the spirit with their natural eyes. You must use your spiritual eyes to see, or discern, strongholds. You must use your spiritual eyes or spiritual discernment to engage in spiritual warfare.

I heard a line of a gospel song one day that said something about the singer seeing his mother on her knees. What was she doing? She was praying. She was engaging in spiritual warfare. The weapons of our warfare are not carnal, but mighty through God through the pulling down of strongholds. Strongholds are vain imaginations. Second Corinthians 10:5 says, "Cast down every vain imagination and high thing that exalts itself against the knowledge of God." A vain imagination is a lie that you believe about God, other people or yourself that exalts itself against the true knowledge of God. A vain imagination is something you believe that is against God's Word.

John 4:23 says that those who worship God must worship Him in spirit and in truth. If you believe a lie about God, you will not worship Him in truth. If you are not fully convinced about the truth of God's Word, you will not see yourself or other people truthfully.

When we are born we are born with a sin nature. The sin nature in itself is a lie. The sin nature says, "I am my own person," but the truth is you are not your own person. Isaiah 45:9 says, "Shall the clay say to him that fashioneth it, What makest thou?" God made us and He knows what is best for us.

We can easily see the sin nature in young children. They can lie very easily. Two-year-olds declare everything to be theirs and the truth is that not everything is theirs. Parents must train their children in truthfulness at a very young age because the stronghold of unbelief – not being convinced of the truth - is hard to overcome.

Some people believe that they can't force change, but they don't believe that change is possible with God's help. We are not to throw our hands up and surrender to the curse of disunity. We are not to be dismayed (II Chron. 20:15). However, to receive God's help we need to believe God. Proverbs 3:5-6 says, "Trust in the Lord with all of your heart and lean not to your own understanding. Acknowledge Him in all of your ways and He will direct your steps." With so many people believing in a form of God, God can seem small or not as significant. Yet He is the creator of all people (Gen. 1:27). He made heaven and earth (Gen. 1:1). God is significant. He is All Mighty (Prov. 24:8). He is great and worthy to be praised (Ps. 18:3).

There Is Only One God

Many people do not have unity in their families because they do not honor God all of the time. There are some people who only honor God on Sundays. There are other people who only honor God on Easter. But God wants to be honored 24 hours a day, 7 days a week, 365 days a year.

Many times we try to put God with our other stuff. Our children also try to put God with their other stuff. I remember when my son was six years old that we had a TV-free week. A TV-free week is a week (about five days) when we do not watch any TV. We fast TV for a week. Well, we had TV-free times before, but we had not had one since our son had turned six. Consequently, it was quite an ordeal when I made it known that we were having a TV-free week. It took my husband and me by surprise when we realized how attached our son had become to the TV. After the announcement he cried. After he cried and cried and cried, he realized crying was not going to change our minds and he found something else he could do. No harm done.

We know our son loves God more than the TV. We know he loves us more than TV, but very quickly he had made the TV an idol. Some people think an idol is a little statue that someone bows downs to. But an idol is anything that stands between us and God. An idol is anything that turns our affection away from God and His Word.

An idol can be a created thing, like the TV, or a created being. Satan is a created being. He told Jesus that if He would bow down and worship him, he would greatly honor Him in the eyes of the world (Matt. 4:9). Satan wants people to bow down to him. He wants people to believe that they will receive great honor apart from God. However, Satan is the one who wants your family destroyed. Still, there are many people who cooperate with the devil on purpose. They are in unity with demonic forces. Some of your family members may transcendental meditate, read their horoscopes, call a psychic, play with an Ouija board, or participate in a cult. Some of your family members are running from God. Some are persecuting preachers. Godly unity will be impossible with these people if they don't change. Godly unity will be impossible with these people if the strongholds over their lives are not broken.

Remember, strongholds are satanic lies that we believe that are against God's Word. Strongholds are in the spiritual realm. Idols are in the natural realm. Sometimes we can turn something good into an idol and not realize it. We can make our children idols. If something bad happens to them and we just can't get over it, we have made them idols. If something good happens to them and we just can't get over it, we have made them idols. The Lord God is One and Him only shall thy worship (Deut. 6:4).

Some people worship their bodies. Anything their bodies want their bodies get. The body could want to overeat or fornicate and the people give in. Some people worship their bodies by exercising a lot. Yet many of those people do not exercise their spirits to the degree they exercise their bodies and we are called to live in the spirit (Gal. 5:25). They put their bodies first. However, there is a balance. We should exercise our bodies. We can get very stiff if we don't. Still we should not exercise our bodies more than we do our spirits. We may exercise our bodies two or three days a week, but we should exercise our spirits all day, every day.

We exercise our spirits through prayer. Some people only want a little bit of God. They only want to pray to Him a little bit. They don't want to bother God. But prayer is not something we should be modest about. We are not bothering God when we pray. First Thessalonians 5:17 says, "Pray without ceasing." Prayer should be as natural to you as breathing. In prayer we give Him all of us and He gives us the part of Him that we can handle. Our giving ourselves to God does not change God, but God giving Himself to us changes us.

God knows the parts of us that need to change. He knows the times when we are trying to change things on our own. We are not to try to change things on our own. We are to be spirit-led people. God's spirit is supposed to guide us and His spirit is not limited to preachers. God did not just make the preachers spiritual beings. He made everyone a spiritual being.

Ministry Helpers Are in Place

That doesn't mean that we don't listen to the preacher. We should listen to the preacher and it is good if we know a preacher personally. A preacher is a person who proclaims the Word of God. Moses was a godly leader. He taught the people the Word of God. Miriam and Aaron came against Moses' leadership. Miriam had to be healed from leprosy. Korah came against Moses' leadership. The earth swallowed him up. Second Chronicles 20:20 says, "Believe in the Lord your God, and you will be established; believe His prophets and you will prosper." The opposite can also be said that if you don't believe the Lord's commandments, you will not be established, and if you don't believe His messengers, you will not prosper.

If you don't believe the commandment to honor thy father and mother, the blessing of unity will not be established in your family. Ultimately, the Word of God is the final authority and God has placed people in the world to proclaim the Word of the Lord. There are authorities in the realm of the spirit. In order for our prayers to be heard, we must walk in submission to spiritual authorities. Ephesians 4:11-13 (KJV) says:

> And he gave some, apostles; and some, prophets; and some, evangelists; and some, pastors and teachers; for the perfecting of the saints, for the work of the ministry, for the edifying of the body of Christ: till we all come in the unity of the faith, and of the knowledge of the Son of God, unto a perfect man, unto the measure of the stature of the fullness of Christ.

The purpose of any spiritual position is to help the saints (the people of God) come to the unity of the faith. The unity of the faith is the position that we as the body of Christ are striving to attain. A person who is in a spiritual position is one who tries to fully convince Christians about the Word of God. As you read this book, I beseech you, have no doubts that God's Word is true and have no doubts that God wants your family and your church family to walk in unity. I also beseech you to pray without ceasing to have a peaceful life (I Thess. 5:17, I Tim. 2:2).

We need a Prayer Life

When we get too focused on our natural lives, the Bible says the cares of this life have stolen the Word (Mark 4:19). We are to maintain our lives. We are to clean the house. We are to work at a job. Still, we are not to focus all of our time on our natural lives and very little time, if any, on our spiritual lives. We shouldn't focus on one or the other. We should focus on both (II Pet. 1:3). The majority of our time will be spent maintaining our natural lives. Yet we must spend quantity and quality time in prayer. We must spend time in prayer to achieve family unity.

The reality, of course, is that we can't spend all of our time in prayer. However, the power of prayer is that after you spend some time in prayer you will spend the rest of your time in your natural life more wisely. God is interested in our whole life, which is both natural and spiritual. Matthew 6:33 says seek first the kingdom of God and all the things we need will be given to us. When we take care of what God cares about, He will take care of what we care about. God cares about our families and wants to help us have family unity.

When we pray for our families, God will take care of our families. Romans 8:31 says if God is for us who can be against us? If God is for us, there is nothing that can stop our families from being blessed. When God is for us there is nothing that can stop us or our children from being blessed (Ps. 115:14). When God is for us all things are possible. All things are possible to us when we pray! (Mark 10:27).

Prayer is a simple act. You can do it anywhere and almost at any time. Yet the enemy will try to do everything he can to prevent you from praying. He'll make you too sleepy or too busy. He'll have people call during your prayer time or one of your kids get up unusually early. He does not want you to talk to God about your family. The devil wants to keep your mind so focused on this natural life, your body, your emotions, the house, or the car, that you are unable to hear God give you the spiritual insight you need to know about your family.

God wants to talk to you about your family. God wants to show Himself strong on your behalf in your family (II Chron. 16:9). Jesus said, "Seek and you will find, knock and the door will open, ask and it will be given to you" (Matt. 7:7). When you ask for your children to be saved and walk in unity with you, the Bible says you will receive what you ask for (Matt. 11:24). Some of you may read this and say, "I have asked for unity with my children and they are still not walking in unity with me." Well, let me ask you: After you prayed, did you love them, nourish a God-inspired vision within them, and nurture them? When you pray God will show you what to do to encourage unity from your family members. He will show you what they need.

Remain at Peace

In order for there to be disunity, something is missing and it may take time to understand what is missing. It may take time to understand what they need and at different seasons of life they may have more needs. Therefore, after you have prayed for your family, you will have to continually maintain your desire for unity. Unity is not something you will ask for one time in your family and expect there never be anymore confusing behaviors, selfish ambition or unrighteous anger. But you can expect to remain at peace.

We can pray for peace. Ephesians 4:3 says that peace is the bond of the Spirit. In our house we understand peace to mean that a person – child or adult – is not mad, not sad, not crying, or whining. I know when I am in the store with my children sometimes they will become "wild." You parents know what I mean. They become hyper, touching everything, bouncing everywhere and I want them to just settle down. I want them to just stop it. They are disturbing my peace.

Sometimes to choose not to lose my peace, we simply have to reduce our time in the store. My children are too tired or too hungry and do not have the strength to keep going. Other times I can simply pray and ask God to give my children peace and they receive it. How do I know they receive it? They calm down. It was a revelation to me to understand that when I am at peace I am calm. I am not mad, yelling or fuming, even though I could be. I am not sad, mourning, or grieving even though I could be. I am not crying, dismayed or upset even though I could be. I am not whining, nagging or blaming even though I could be. I am at peace. Psalms 131:2 says like a weaned child, I have learned to quiet my soul.

Because I have been diligent to have peace, I have peaceful children. Hebrews 4:11 encourages us to be diligent to enter into God's rest, God's peace. I heard Pastor Benny Hinn say that when God moves on a person that person will be quiet or calm. In the Bible when Jesus showed up on the scene the demons shrieked, but when they were cast out of the people, the people were calm (Mark 5:1-15, Mark 1:23-27, Mark 7: 25-30, Luke 9:42). When the wind and the waves acted up, Jesus said, "Peace, be still...and there was a great calm" (Mark 4:39).

When the enemy is pushed away from us, we will have great peace in our families. Remember, it is not your children, spouse or parents that are stealing your peace, driving you crazy or anything like that. It is the devil. Ephesians 6:12 says we wrestle not against flesh and blood, but against powers, principalities, rulers in high places. These spiritual enemies are fighting you to steal your peace and prevent your family from walking in unity.

The unity principles of love, nourishment and nurture when naturally applied should greatly improve your relationships. Honoring your father and mother will bring great peace to your natural life. Yet prayer exposes the spiritual strongholds. Praying for your family and praying with your family will enable you to hear from God and defeat the spiritual enemies that attempt to steal your family's peace and disunite your family.

Let Us Pray

Prayer is not hard. A child to an elderly person can do it and should do it. Stormie Omartian has written several excellent how-to-pray books for the family and I encourage you to learn all you can about praying for your family.

Breaking a curse off your family is not just a matter of will power. It is not just a matter of positive thinking. It isn't just a matter of renewing your mind to follow a five-step plan of how to walk in unity. Breaking the curse of disunity off of your life is a matter of spending time with God so He can show you specific things to do to maintain unity in your family. He can forewarn you about things that would destroy unity in your family. He can show you that your child's misbehavior is simply a lack of love, a lack of nurturing, or a lack of nourishment.

God speaks. Many times when we pray we do all of the talking, but we need to listen to Him. Hebrews 11:6 says you have to come to God in faith believing that He is and that He is the rewarder of those who seek Him. In other words, when you come to Him expect Him to speak to you.

In Matthew 6 Jesus taught the disciples how to come to God. He taught them how to pray. We can pray the model, but the model just shows us how to pray, not the exact words to say every time we pray. Matthew 6:9-13 (KJV) says, "After this manner therefore pray ye:

<u>Our Father which art in heaven, Hallowed be thy name.</u>
When we begin to pray we should first acknowledge that God is God. By that I mean we want to say that we know who we are talking to. When we talk to our parents we call them by name, Mom, Dad. When we pray we call God by His name, "Father."

After calling on God we acknowledge one of His attributes. In the Lord's Prayer, Jesus acknowledges God's holiness. He says "hallowed" or holy is Your name. When we pray we could acknowledge His mercy or His love. When you pray acknowledge some of God's attributes.

<u>Thy kingdom come. Thy will be done in earth, as it is in heaven.</u>
Acknowledge that He is the King of kings and we are part of His kingdom. Heaven is where His kingdom is. Earth is where we are. We want the same unity on earth as it is in heaven. In heaven everyone knows they are loved. In heaven everyone is spiritually strong. In heaven everyone does their job of worshipping God. In heaven there is no disunity.

<u>Give us this day our daily bread.</u>
Ask God for bread. God has provided everything we need to walk in unity. He has provided "the bread" for our behavior. The bread needed to walk in unity is creativity. We need to be creative people in order to get out of the rut of disunity. God can fill us with the creativity of loving others instead of confusing them. He can fill us with the creativity of nurturing others instead of being angry with them. He can fill us with the creativity of nourishing others instead of being selfish. God is a creative God. He wants us to be creative people.

And forgive us our debts, as we forgive our debtors.

Jesus says to ask for forgiveness for our debts. It is interesting that He did not say, "Forgive us for our sins." He means sins, but He says, "...forgive us our debts." A debt in the spirit is the same thing as a debt in the natural. It is a charge that we cannot pay. A debt in the natural is money we owe. A debt against God is one we can't pay in the spirit.

There are times when we know that we have blown it. We have missed the mark. We have disobeyed God. We know we are wrong. When we sin we go into debt. Jesus paid for our sins. He paid our debts. Yet He pays for our debts as we pay for those who have debts against us. He only forgives our sins as we forgive our parents or as we forgive our children.

One of life's greatest disappointments is when our parents and/or children do not share our faith. We expect them to agree with us and they don't. We expect them to see what we can see and they don't. We expect them to understand...and they don't. This causes unintentional hurts. We must forgive them and continue to pray that the eyes of their understanding be opened (Eph. 1:18).

When we have the unity of the faith great power is available to our families. Deuteronomy 32:30 says one can put a thousand to flight and two can put ten thousand to flight. When our families walk in the disunity of the faith, we do not have all the power God has made available to us. When the family does not walk in the unity of the faith, everyone is not spiritually focused. Faith calls those things that are not, to be things that are (Rom. 4:17). Faith sees something in the spirit and calls it into the natural.

When there is disunity of the faith, everyone is not carrying their weight of the spiritual life in the family. When there is disunity of the faith, everyone cannot see in the spirit. My mother is a pioneer. She was one of the first people in our family to be born again. She was one of the first people in our family to live for God. She carried the weight of our spiritual lives in prayer for many years. She had to forgive her children for dishonoring her. Of course, in the natural course of life, forgiveness must be given. But when a family member is walking in the disunity of the faith, she does not easily repent. She does not "see" that she is wrong.

A person who is walking in the unity of the faith will repent. He may have been disrespectful, but he will also be repentant when he realizes what he has done is wrong. A person who is walking in the unity of the faith does not want to break the unity of the faith. Faith is a complex subject because we go from faith to faith. There are different levels of faith (Rom. 1:17). Jesus said there is great faith, little faith and no faith (Matt. 8:10, Matt. 8:26, Mark 4:40). When there is no faith, your family is obviously not walking in the unity of the faith. Yet even among saved family members, there still can be areas of no faith. Disunity of the faith can be present among Christians, but because we profess Christ it may not be as obvious.

A lack of faith brings about disunity of the faith. Jesus asked when the Son of Man returns will He find faith in the earth (Luke 18:8). As Christians, everything we do we are to do by faith and we need to do everything in our power to increase our faith. Daily prayer along with daily reading through the Bible will increase your faith. Many people do not read through their Bible (Acts 20:27). They read the familiar Bible stories, but they do not know the whole counsel of the Word of God. We need to know God's Word in order to know the promises. As we know the promise, we can stand on the promises. As we stand on the promises, we will increase our faith. Other ways we can increase our faith include: reading this book, reading other faith-filled books, being saved and water baptized, completing a discipleship course, attending a Bible school or obtaining a theological degree. When we fail to reach out to increase our faith we have encountered disunity of the faith. Remember, faith should be ever-increasing.

Our faith is the key to unlock the door to what we receive. Some people receive 30-fold of God's promise. Some people receive 60-fold of God's promise. Still others receive 100-fold of God's promise. Maybe you have faith for unity with your parents (30). Maybe you have faith for unity with your parents and spouse (60). But suppose you have faith for unity with your parents, spouse and children (100). Matthew 9:29 says it will be to you according to your faith.

<u>And lead us not into temptation, but deliver us from evil: For thine is the kingdom, and the power, and the glory, for ever. Amen.</u>

We break the unity of the faith when we are led into the temptation of evil. When we ask God not to lead us into temptation, we are asking him not to lead us into confusing behaviors, selfish ambition or unrighteous anger. We ask Him to deliver us from demonic strongholds and everything that would lead to disunity. Romans 12:21 says not to be overcome with evil, but overcome evil with good. When we are delivered from the curse of disunity we will overcome it with the blessings of unity. We will overcome confusing behaviors, selfish ambition and unrighteous anger by loving, nurturing and nourishing our family members.

Finally, when we end our prayer, we must remember to thank God for His goodness in our lives. We must remember to acknowledge His great power and His mighty deeds on behalf of men. We must remember to tell people that it is because of God's mighty hand on our lives that our family is able to walk in unity. God deserves all the credit and the glory for supplying the power we need to break the curse of disunity.

As we come to the conclusion of this book, I pray that you will have more blessed and stable relationships. I pray that you do not stop loving your family. I look forward to hearing your testimony of how this book has helped your family in any way and remember: How good and pleasant it is when the brothers dwell in unity...for there God has commanded the blessing (Ps. 133:1-3) and honor your father and mother and it will be well with you (Ex. 20:12).

Here is a prayer that you can recite to help you and your family to walk in unity.

Father God, You are good and Your mercy endures forever. I ask You to pour Your love into my heart. Pour it in to over flowing. Help me to see my family the way that You do. Help me not to judge them, but love them. Show me how to minister Your love to each one of them.

Father, in Jesus' Name I ask You to strengthen me. Fill me with Your strength in my inner man. I don't want to turn to the left or the right from the path of unity. Father, I forgive my parents, my spouse, my children and my siblings for rejecting, criticizing, or being impatient with me. I forgive them for acting selfishly with their time or things. I forgive them for the times they have used their anger to hurt me. Please forgive me for the times that I have rejected, criticized, or acted impatiently with them. Please forgive me for acting selfishly with my time or my things. Please forgive me for times I have used my anger to hurt my family. I thank You for forgiving me and making me strong in You.

Lord, I also ask that You fill me with the knowledge of Your will for my life. Open the eyes of my understanding that I may know the hope of my calling. I thank You for opening doors of opportunities for me to use my gifts and talents. I thank You for opening doors of opportunities for my family to use their gifts and talents. I thank You for supplying all of my and my family's needs. I thank You for making all grace abound toward me and my family so that we will always, having all sufficiency in all things, abound to every good work.

I break every demonic stronghold in my life and my family's lives. I declare my family is alive with Christ. Old things have passed away and all things have become new. Thank You, Lord, for a new way for me to relate to my family and for them to relate to me. In Jesus' Name we walk in unity. Lord, You are the only wise God forever and ever. Thank You for loving me and my family in Jesus' Name, Amen.

Pamela Ellis is a native of Durham, North Carolina. She is married to a loving husband, Otha, and has three wonderful children, Andrew, Annalise and Angelea.

Pamela is a graduate of Oral Roberts University. She has worked with preschool children for many years and has a heart to see families living out God's purpose.

To contact the author, please write:

Pamela Ellis
P.O. Box 701242
Tulsa, OK 74170

Printed in the United States
130240LV00002B/4/P

9 781606 477601